# EDGAR ALLAN POE

## His Life, Letters, and Opinions

BY

## JOHN H. INGRAM

"Unhappy Master whom unmerciful Disaster
Followed fast and followed faster till his songs one burden bore—
Till the dirges of his Hope that melancholy burden bore
Of 'Never—nevermore.'"

With Portraits of Poe and his Mother.

VOL. I.

## LONDON:
### JOHN HOGG, PATERNOSTER ROW
&c.

All rights reserved

## Printing Statement:

Due to the very old age and scarcity of this book, many of the pages may be hard to read due to the blurring of the original text, possible missing pages, missing text, dark backgrounds and other issues beyond our control.

Because this is such an important and rare work, we believe it is best to reproduce this book regardless of its original condition.

Thank you for your understanding.

EDGAR ALLAN POE

FROM A PHOTOGRAPH

# PREFACE.

———o———

At last, after several years of research, I am enabled
to place a full and faithful life of Edgar Allan Poe
before the world. It was due to myself, due to the
public, and due to the memory of a much maligned
man, that the short, vindicatory "Memoir" prefixed to
my edition of Poe's Works in 1874,* and my essays
on his Life and Works—published before and after
that sketch—should culminate in such a work as this.
When that "Memoir of Poe" was published, I drew
attention to the fact that no trustworthy biography
of the poet had yet appeared in his own country,
although that such a work had been frequently projected was then pointed out. Since the publication
of my sketch, however, and its substitution in
America for Griswold's so-called "Memoir of Poe,"

* Edinburgh : A. & C. Black. 4 vols.

quite a plentiful supply of "Original" lives of the poet have appeared, and all—save one "based upon Griswold's sketch"—have reproduced the whole of my material, without acknowledgment, and with scarcely an additional item of interest or value.

My sketch, above referred to, having accomplished its purpose of proving that the obloquy overshadowing the poet's moral character arose chiefly from the almost unparalleled hostility of his earliest biographer, it has not been deemed requisite in the following pages to allude, save slightly and incidentally, to the mythology of scandal which has grown up about Poe's story.

In preparing this final work upon Edgar Allan Poe, I have found no lack of new matter: the quality rather than the quantity of the proffered *data* has been my chief hindrance. To perceive how folk a man scarcely knew, and probably detested, will claim —and almost beyond power of refutation—to have enjoyed his friendly intimacy; to have supplied him with ideas; to have suggested his themes, and even to have written his works, is quite appalling. They misrepresent his idlest words; distort his most trivial remarks—perchance unintentionally; falsify dates, invent anecdotes; fabricate conversations, and, indeed, refrain from nothing, in order to prove their acquaintance with departed genius. The amount of mischief that can be, and is, manufactured out of a dead man's relics is terrible. Woe betide the luckless mortal who leaves a history! Vivisection is merciful compared with the pitilessness of the *post-mortem* examination held upon his real and putative remains!

Having learned all this, it would, indeed, have been a satisfaction to me to have felt assured that I had steered clear of all such unreliable gossip or malicious invention, and that my many years' labour and research had culminated in such a work as Poe, in his reviewal of Carlyle's *Life of Schiller*, portrays: "This biography is not merely a sketch of the poet's life. . . . It is a gradual development of his heart and mind, of his nature as a poet and a man, that endears him more to us, while it enables us more thoroughly to comprehend him. We can trace here the growth of his faculties, and his progress amidst the struggles and obstacles of his early career; from the time when his 'strong untutored spirit,' consumed by its own activity, was chafing blindly, like ocean waves, against the barriers that restrained it—through diffi-

culties and vexations which only his burning energy
of soul enabled him to overcome—up to that calm,
intellectual elevation, in the lucid expansion of which
he could watch the workings of his imagination, and
subject the operations of his genius to the requisitions
of taste."

In bidding farewell to what has engrossed so much
of my life and labour, it is both pleasant and just that
I should offer my grateful thanks to those who have
so generously and so assiduously worked with me.
To books my indebtedness as regards this "Life" is
slight; few, beyond the " Edgar Poe and his Critics "
of the late Mrs. Whitman, having been of any service
to me: to that dear friend and fellow-worker my
obligations are manifold and heavy.   To the late Mrs.
Houghton—the poet's "Marie Louise"—my affectionate gratitude is stronger than words; to "Annie"—
the poet's own "Annie"—and to Mrs. Shelton, I am
greatly beholden, as, also, to "Stella" and to Mrs. Gove-
Nichols.   To Professor James Wood Davidson I am
much indebted, both for material and aid, as likewise
to Mr. E. V. Valentine, the Virginian sculptor; to my
friend, Dr. W. Hand Browne of Baltimore, and to the
late brave old John Neal, who, like so many fellow-

workers, has not stayed to see the completion of our labour. To the Poes of Baltimore, for correction of *data*, and copies of correspondence, my thanks are due; and to Mr. William Wertenbaker, and the Chairman and Faculty of the University of Virginia, and the late Professors T. Hewitt Key and George Long; to Colonel John T. Preston, for the use of his interesting reminiscences; to the authorities of West Point Military Academy; to Dr. N. H. Morison and Mr. John Parker of the Peabody Institute, Baltimore, and to all the many friends and correspondents—known and unknown—who have aided me in this work, my most sincere thanks are now heartily tendered.

JOHN H. INGRAM.

London, *May* 1880.

# BIOGRAPHICAL DATA.

—o—

January 19, 1809. Born at Boston, Massachusetts.

December 8, 1811. His mother died at Richmond, Virginia.

       ,,    [Edgar Poe adopted by Mr. John Allan.]

1816. Brought to Europe, and placed at school in Stoke Newington.

1821. Returns to the United States.

1822. Placed at school in Richmond, Virginia.

February 1, 1826. Enters University of Virginia.

[Signs matriculation book, 14th February 1836.]

December 15, 1826. Leaves University of Virginia.

1827. "Tamerlane and Other Poems" printed at Boston.

June ? 1827. Departs for Europe.

March, 1829. Returns to Richmond, Virginia.

       ,,    Publishes "Al Aaraaf, Tamerlane, and Minor Poems," at Baltimore.

July 1, 1830. Admitted as cadet to West Point Military Academy.

March 6, 1831. Dismissed the Military Academy.

     ,,    ,,    Publishes "Poems," New York.

Autumn, 1833. Gains prize from *Saturday Visiter* (Baltimore).

December, 1835. Editor of the *Southern Literary Messenger* (Richmond, Virginia).

| | | |
|---|---|---|
| May 16, | 1836. | Married to his cousin, Virginia Clemm, at Richmond. [Virginia C. born August 13th, 1822.] |
| January, | 1837. | Resigns editorship of *Southern Literary Messenger.* |
| | 1837–8. | Resides in New York. |
| July, | 1838. | "Arthur Gordon Pym" published, New York and London. |
| Autumn, | 1838. | Removes to Philadelphia. |
| July, | 1839. | Editor of the *Gentleman's Magazine*, Philadelphia. |
| | 1840. | "Tales of the Grotesque and Arabesque" published, Philadelphia. |
| | 1840. | "The Conchologist's First Book" published, Philadelphia. |
| June, | ,, | Resigns editorship of *Gentleman's Magazine.* |
| January, | 1841. | Editor of *Graham's Magazine*, Philadelphia. |
| April, | 1842. | Resigns editorship of *Graham's Magazine.* |
| Spring, | 1843. | Gains $100 prize for "The Gold Bug." |
| Autumn, | 1844. | Sub-editor of the *Evening Mirror*, New York. |
| January 29, | 1845. | "The Raven" published in *Evening Mirror.* |
| February 28, | 1845. | Lectures in New York Historical Society's room. |
| March 8, | ,, | Joint-editor of the *Broadway Journal.* |
| July, | ,, | "Tales" published, New York and London. |
| ,, | ,, | Sole-editor of the *Broadway Journal.* |
| November 1, | ,, | Proprietor of *Broadway Journal.* |
| ,, | ,, | "The Raven and Other Poems" published, New York and London. |
| Winter, | ,, | Lectures at Boston Lyceum. |
| December, | ,, | *Broadway Journal* disposed of. |
| February, | 1846. | "The Literati" begun in Godey's *Lady's Book.* |
| June 23, | ,, | *Evening Mirror* publishes libel. |
| ,, 28, | ,, | "Reply" to libel in Philadelphia *Saturday Gazette.* |
| Summer, | ,, | Removes to Fordham. |

January 30, 1847. His wife dies.

February 17, ,, Gains libel suit against *Evening Mirror.*

February 3, 1848. Lectures in New York Historical Society's room.

Summer, ,, "Eureka" published, New York.

,, ,, Richmond, Virginia, revisited.

,, ,, Lectures at Lowell, Mass., and Providence, R.I.

October, ,, Betrothed to Mrs. Whitman.

December, ,, Engagement with Mrs. Whitman broken off.

June 30, 1849. Departs for the South.

Autumn, ,, In Richmond and neighbourhood.

October 7, ,, Dies at Baltimore, Maryland.

November 17, 1875. Monument Inaugurated, Baltimore.

# CONTENTS OF VOLUME I.

————o————

# EDGAR ALLAN POE.

## CHAPTER I.

### *PARENTAGE.*

EDGAR ALLAN POE was of gentle birth.* His paternal grandfather, General David Poe, the descendant
of an ancient and highly connected family, was
born in Ireland, but, taken at a very early age by
his parents to the United States, became a patriotic
citizen of his adopted country, and greatly distinguished himself during the War of Independence. The
General's eldest son, David, was destined for the law,
and after receiving the usual quantum of education
then afforded by the schools of Baltimore—his birthplace — was placed under Mr. William Gwynn,
barrister-at-law, to read for the bar.

The youthful student, the future poet's father,
would appear to have found greater attraction in

---

* *Vide* Appendix A, for *Ancestry.*

the drama than in jurisprudence, and, according to the testimony of a fellow-townsman,[*] "young Poe and several of his gay companions formed an association called the 'Thespian Club,' for the promotion of a taste for the drama. They met in a large room, in a house belonging to General Poe. . . . Here, at their weekly meetings, they recited passages from the old dramatists, and performed the popular plays of the day, for the entertainment of themselves and their friends." According to the same authority, "David Poe became so infatuated with the stage that he secretly left his home in Baltimore, and went to Charleston, where he was announced to make his 'first appearance on any stage.' One of his uncles, William Poe, . . . saw the announcement in the newspapers; he went to Charleston, took David off the stage, and put him in the law office of the Honourable John Forsyth of Augusta," Georgia, his own (William Poe's) brother-in-law.

The veritable cause of David's escapade would appear to have been something even stronger than an infatuation for the stage. Whilst still studying law under Mr. Gwynn, young Poe was sent to Norfolk, Virginia, upon professional business, and there saw and became deeply enamoured of Elizabeth Arnold, a youthful and beautiful English actress. From Norfolk the

---

[*] E. L. Didier, *Life of Edgar A. Poe*, pp. 23, 24.

company to which Miss Arnold was attached migrated
to Charleston, whither, apparently, it was followed by
the young lady's admirer. Different reasons have
been given to account for the youthful couple's temporary and compulsory separation; but, whatever may
have been the facts, they speedily met again, and
ultimately were married, the bridegroom being but
nineteen, and the bride about the same age. David
Poe's parents were incensed at the imprudent match,
and forbade him the house; and as neither he nor his
wife possessed any means of subsistence, they turned
to the stage in search of a livelihood.

Many absurd stories have been retailed as to the
parentage of Elizabeth Arnold, one widely-circulated
rumour declaring her to have been the daughter of
General Benedict Arnold, the American traitor. The
facts are not yet thoroughly known, but it is believed
that her father was an Englishman of very good
family, though in impoverished circumstances, who
sought refuge in the United States, where he endeavoured to support himself by literature. Elizabeth
Arnold herself was born at sea, where her mother is
supposed to have died at, or directly after, the child's
birth. The little girl being left fatherless, as well as
motherless, whilst still an infant, was, apparently,
adopted by some compassionate stranger, and carefully
educated for the stage. Eventually the poor little

orphaned foreigner made her appearance in public, her *début* as an actress taking place on August 18th, 1797, at the old John Street Theatre, New York, in the juvenile character of "Maria," in the farce of *The Spoiled Child.*[*] Two nights later she appeared as "Agnes," in the tragedy of *The Mountaineers*, and is recorded to have made a very favourable impression by her youth, her beauty, and her precocious ability. Mr. Solee, a well-known *impresario* of the period, engaged the juvenile *débutante* for a company he was forming, and under his management, and that of his successors, Messrs. Williamson, Placide, and others, the young English girl became an accomplished actress, ultimately appearing in the leading *rôles* of the tragic drama. Between her first appearance on the New York stage, and her reappearance there in 1806 as Mrs. David Poe, Miss Arnold's career may be traced at the various theatres of New York, Philadelphia, Norfolk, and Charleston; and it is pleasant to hear her talented son, in the brightest epoch of his own short life, when alluding to his mother's profession, declare that "no earl was ever prouder of his earldom than he of his descent from a woman who, although well born, hesitated not to consecrate to the drama her brief career of genius and beauty."

[*] Ireland, *Records of the New York Stage*, vol. i. p. 42.

In 1806, when Mrs. Poe reappeared in New York, she was accompanied by her husband. The youthful couple were engaged at the new Vauxhall Garden, where the lady made her *entrée* on the 16th of July, as "Priscilla," in *The Tomboy*, whilst Mr. Poe made his first appearance on the New York stage on the 18th, as "Frank," in *Fortune's Frolic.* "The lady was young and pretty," remarks Ireland, "and evinced talent both as singer and actress ; the gentleman was literally nothing." * Eventually the Poes removed from New York to Boston, where they frequently performed. Their various appearances on the stage at the latter city may be traced in 1808 from the commencement of April until the 3rd of June, the theatre having been opened on the latter date for "one night only," in honour of the time renowned "Artillery Election." A noteworthy circumstance, both for the calculators of prenatal influences, and the analytic student of Poe's works, is that on the 18th of April 1808—just nine months before the poet's birth—Mr. and Mrs. Poe appeared in Schiller's ominous tragedy of *The Robbers*, and were assisted by their old friends, Mr. and Mrs. Usher. Their thoughts are likely to have been more than usually occupied with the selection of the piece for performance, as it was their benefit night, and, apparently their own

* *Records of the New York Stage.*

speculation, they having announced, "That from the great failure and severe losses sustained by their former attempts, they [the Poes and the Ushers] have been induced to make a joint effort." The *rôle* of " Amelia " was assigned to Mrs. Poe, who, towards the end of her brief career, almost invariably undertook the chief female characters, whilst her husband's impersonations strangely varied from the leading male down to the most minor personages of the drama.

What became of the Poes during the summer, or what they did for a livelihood until the winter season of 1808-9 commenced, can only be conjectured. Other means of subsistence than those derived from their dramatic labours may have been provided by Mrs. Poe's abilities : she was an accomplished artist, and left one or two sketches that have been much admired.    One of her paintings, that ultimately came into the possession of her celebrated son, was a view of " Boston  Harbour : Morning, 1808 ; " and upon the back of it was inscribed, in a neatly-written round hand, not very dissimilar from the poet's own beautiful caligraphy, a description ending with the words, " For my little son Edgar, who should ever love Boston, the place of his birth, and where his mother found her best and most sympathetic friends."

During the winter of 1808-9, the Poes frequently

appeared on the Boston boards. On the 17th of January, Mrs. Poe was absent from the performance, and on the 19th, her second son, Edgar, was born. In less than a month the young mother reappeared, and continued playing in Boston until the 19th of April, when she took her benefit, assuming the Shakesperian *rôles* of "Ophelia" and "Cordelia," whilst her husband, whose health was probably breaking, had to content himself with the minor character of "Laertes." Upon this occasion, as also upon many others, Mrs. Poe sang "a favourite song."

At the close of the Boston season the young couple, after paying a short visit to Baltimore in order to fetch their little boy from General Poe's, where he was staying, flitted back to New York. On the 6th of September they appeared at the Park Theatre of that city, in *The Castle Spectre*, as "Hassan and Angela." * They wintered in New York, remaining there until the beginning of July, when they removed to Richmond, Virginia, where, it is believed, early in 1811, David Poe died of consumption. Some months after their father's decease a third child, Rosalie, was born. Mrs. Poe's own health now began to fail rapidly, and in consequence of her inability to continue her professional engagements, her circumstances became truly deplorable. These facts becoming known, certain

* Dunlop, *History of the American Stage*, vol. ii. p. 265.

ladies interested themselves on her behalf, and minis-
tered to her wants.   A Mrs. Richards and other Richmond ladies who visited the dying actress, frequently
commented, in a manner that has left a lasting impression, upon Mrs. Poe's evident refinement of manner;
and, despite her poverty and sickness, the exquisite
neatness of herself and her surroundings.   All help,
however, was now of slight avail, for on Sunday the
8th of December, the unfortunate lady followed her
husband to the tomb, like him dying of decline.   On
the Tuesday following her death, the *Richmond En-
quirer* contained this announcement :—

  " DIED.—On Sunday last, Mrs. Poe, one of the actresses
of the company at present playing on the Richmond Boards.
By the death of this Lady the Stage has been deprived of
one of its chief ornaments.   And to say the least of her, she
was an interesting Actress, and never failed to catch the
applause, and command the admiration, of the beholder."

Beyond the fleeting memory of her beauty and
talent, Mrs. Poe left little for her three fatherless
children ; but, in after years, the sketches above referred
to, and a parcel of her letters, were cherished by her
illustrious son, among his most highly-valued treasures.
Evidently she was a woman of great intellectual
capacity, as is indeed displayed in her portrait by a
breadth of brow similar to that possessed by Edgar
Poe, and to conceal the masculine appearance of

which she was accustomed to wear her hair low down over her forehead, as shown in the portrait accompanying the second volume.*

Upon the death of their surviving parent, David Poe's three children—in accordance with a custom not unusual in republican countries—were adopted by comparative strangers. Edgar was taken by Mr. John Allan, a wealthy Scotch merchant, married to an American lady and settled in Virginia; William Henry Leonard, the date and place of whose birth is still uncertain, by some relative or friend in Baltimore,† and Rosalie, by the family of another Scotchman named McKenzie.‡

* The miniature from which our portrait is copied, is one that accompanied the poet through all his wanderings. Shortly before his death he gave it to a very valued friend, from whom we received it. A second portrait of Mrs. Poe, it may be remarked, remained in the possession of her famous son until his decease, but its subsequent fate is unknown to us.—J. H. I.

† *Vide* Appendix B.            ‡ *Vide* Appendix C.

## CHAPTER II.

### *CHILDHOOD.*

EDGAR ALLAN POE was born at Boston, on the 19th of January 1809. His parents' professional engagements and restricted means could not have permitted them to give any very cordial welcome to this addition to their limited *ménage*. When the child was only five weeks old it was taken by its parents to Baltimore, and left in the charge of its grandfather's household, where the beauty and talent of its mother appear to have effected a reconciliation between the General and his prodigal son. After staying some months with his relatives in Maryland, Edgar was reclaimed by his parents, and apparently stayed with his mother until her death in 1811.

The poor little orphan is recorded to have already manifested promise of great beauty. At the solicitations of his wife, Mr. John Allan agreed to adopt the boy, who, for several subsequent years, was to be known as Edgar Allan. Mr. Allan, a native of Ayrshire, Scotland, had emigrated to the United

States, and settled in Virginia, where he made a considerable fortune by the purchase and export of tobacco : at the time when he adopted this child he was only thirty-one, although, apparently, he had been already long married. Not only was Edgar a handsome and precocious boy, but he was in some way related to his godfather, who had, therefore, every cause to compassionate the little orphan's condition. In the home of his adoptive parents the boy found much of the luxury wealth could provide, and in the person of Mrs. Allan as much affection as a childless wife could bestow. Edgar won the admiration, even if he did not gain the affection, of Mr. Allan, who became extremely proud of his youthful *protégé*, and treated him in many respects as his own son. Although little that is trustworthy can now be learned of the poet's early days, it is worth record that a tenacious memory and a musical ear are said to have enabled him to learn by rote, and declaim with effect, the finest passages of English poetry, to the evening visitors at his godfather's house. "The justness of his emphasis, and his evident appreciation of the poems he recited, made a striking impression upon his audience, while every heart was won by the ingenuous simplicity and agreeable manners of the pretty little elocutionist." Gratifying as these exhibitions may have been to Mr. Allan's vanity, the probable consequence of such a system of recurring excitements upon the boy's morbidly nervous organisation could scarcely fail to prove injurious. Indeed, in after years, the poet bitterly bewailed the pernicious effects of his childhood's misdirected aims. "I am," he declared, "the descendant of a race whose imaginative and easily excitable temperament has at all times rendered them remarkable; and in my earliest infancy I gave evidence of having fully inherited the family character. As I advanced in years it was more strongly developed, becoming, for many reasons, a cause of serious disquietude to my friends, and of positive injury to myself. . . . My voice was a household law, and, at an age when few children have abandoned their leading strings, I was left to the guidance of my own will, and became, in all but name, the master of my own actions."

After receiving the rudiments of his education in an academy at Richmond, Poe accompanied the Allans to Europe, whither they were called on matters connected with the disposal of some property left to Mr. Allan by a relative. Edgar is supposed to have visited several portions of Great Britain in the company of his adoptive parents, and a sister of Mrs. Allan's. Upon their arrival in London, in 1816, the boy was placed at a school in Stoke Newington, then a distinct town, but now a suburb of the metropolis. Part of the time Edgar was under the charge of the Rev. Dr. Bransby, the Allans resided in the vicinity of Russell

Square, whither every recurring Friday he returned, remaining with them until the following Monday.*

The Rev. Dr. Bransby, afterwards so quaintly portrayed by Poe in his story of *William Wilson,* "is remembered as having had the reputation of being a thorough scholar, very apt at quotation, especially from Shakespeare and Horace," and also as "a strict disciplinarian." When young "Allan," as Edgar was styled, was placed under Dr. Bransby's care, he was found to be "very backward with his studies, not having had any regular instruction;" but when he left the Stoke Newington Manor House School, "he was able to speak French, construe any easy Latin author, and was far better acquainted with history and literature than many boys of a more advanced age, who had had greater advantages than he had." † "Edgar Allan" was described by Dr. Bransby as "a quick and clever boy," who "would have been a very good boy had he not been spoilt by his parents," as he termed the Allans; "but they spoilt him, and allowed him an extravagant amount of pocket-money, which enabled him to get into all manner of mischief. Still I liked the boy," added the schoolmaster; "poor fellow, his parents spoilt him."

To his sojourn in England Poe looked back with

---

\* Mrs. Clemm's Letters to Judge Neilson Poe.
† *Athenæum,* No. 2660, pp. 496–97, October 19, 1878.

anything but ungrateful reminiscences, as a reference
to his tale of *William Wilson* proves. His description of Stoke Newington, as it was when he resided
there, is unusually accurate in its suggestive details.
Many of the features of his school and school-life are
reproduced with a graphicality unequalled anywhere,
save in the parallel records of Balzac's " *Louis Lambert.*"
It is not presuming too much upon the probabilities
to suggest, that much of the gloom and glamour which
pervade Poe's writings originated in the strangeness
and isolation of the lad's position in that foreign and
" excessively ancient house," of that " misty looking
village of England." The dreamy walks, even now
overshadowed by immemorial elms, and the mouldering
dwellings that then abounded—some few remain—in
the vicinity of his English schoolhouse, could not
fail to exercise a marked influence upon a mind so
morbidly sensitive to impressions as was Poe's; nor
can it be doubted that in the *lustrum* of his life there
spent he acquired some portion at least of that
curious and *outré* classic lore which, in after years,
became one of the chief ornaments of his weird
works.

When Poe resided at Stoke Newington the Manor
House school-grounds occupied a very large area; but
of late years, owing to the continuous encroachments
of enterprising builders, they have been much cir-

cumscribed in extent, and the house greatly altered in appearance. The description of the place, as well as the representation of his school-life there, had, the poet declared, been faithfully given in *William Wilson*, but in order to trace out this *vraisemblance*— at least, as regards the building and some minor *data* —the earliest known version of the story must be referred to, subsequent revisions which it afterwards underwent at its author's hands having somewhat detracted from its fidelity to fact. "The large, rambling, Elizabethan house," into which Poe ultimately, and evidently for the purpose of heightening the picturesque effect, metamorphosed the "old, irregular, and cottage-built" dwelling, portrayed more correctly the appearance of a fine old manorial residence that formerly faced the school, but which quite recently has been ruthlessly razed for "improvements."

"In truth," remarks the *soi-disant* "William Wilson," "it was a dream-like and spirit-soothing place, that venerable old town," and it is not strange the boy's plastic mind should have retained, indelibly imprinted upon it, a vivid impression of "the refreshing chilliness of its deeply-shadowed avenues," and, in fancy, "inhale the fragrance of its thousand shrubberies, and thrill anew with indefinable delight at the deep hollow note of the church-bell, breaking each hour, with sullen and sudden roar, upon the stillness of the dusky atmosphere in which the old fretted Gothic steeple lay imbedded and asleep."

Within this dream-engendering place the quondam Edgar Allan spent about five years of his brief existence; and, notwithstanding the apparent monotony of school-life, was doubtless fully justified in looking back upon the days passed in that venerable academy with pleasurable feelings. "The teeming brain of childhood," to repeat Poe's own words, "requires no external world of incident to occupy or amuse it. The morning's awakening, the nightly summons to bed; the connings, the recitations, the periodical half holidays and perambulations; the playground, with its broils, its pastimes, its intrigues—these, by a mental sorcery long forgotten, were made to involve a wilderness of sensation, a world of rich incident, a universe of varied emotion, of excitement the most passionate and spirit-stirring. *'Oh, le bon temps, que ce siècle de fer!'"*

"Old and irregular," as the poet described it, the house still is. "The grounds," he remarks further, "were extensive, and a high and solid brick wall, topped with a bed of mortar and broken glass, encompassed the whole. This prison-like rampart formed the limit of our domain; beyond it we saw but thrice a week—once every Saturday afternoon, when, attended by two ushers, we were permitted to take brief walks in a body through some of the neighbouring fields—and twice during Sunday, when we were paraded in the same formal manner to the morning and evening service in the one church of the village. Of this church the principal of our school was pastor. With how deep a spirit of wonder and perplexity was I wont to regard him from our remote pew in the gallery, as, with step solemn and slow, he ascended the pulpit! This reverend man, with countenance so demurely benign, with robes.so glossy and so clerically flowing, with wig so minutely powdered, so rigid and so vast,—could this be he who, of late, with sour visage, and in snuffy habiliments, administered, ferule in hand, the Draconian laws of the academy? Oh, gigantic paradox, too utterly monstrous for solution!

"At an angle of the ponderous wall frowned a more ponderous gate. It was riveted and studded with iron bolts, and surmounted with jagged iron spikes. What impressions of deep awe did it inspire! It was never opened save for the three periodical egressions and ingressions already mentioned; then, in every creak of its mighty hinges, we found a plenitude of mystery—a world of matter for solemn remark, or for more solemn meditation.

"The extensive enclosure was irregular in form, having many capacious recesses. Of these, three or four of the largest constituted the playground. It was level, and covered with fine hard gravel. I well remember it had no trees, nor benches, nor anything similar within it. Of course it was in the rear of the house. In front lay a small parterre, planted with box and other shrubs; but through this sacred division we passed only upon rare occasions indeed—such as a first advent to school or final departure thence, or perhaps, when a parent or friend having called for us, we joyfully took our way home for the Christmas or Midsummer holidays.

"But the house!—how quaint an old building was this !—

to me how veritably a palace of enchantment! There was
really no end to its windings—to its incomprehensible sub-
divisions. It was difficult, at any given time, to say with
certainty upon which of its two stories one happened to be.
From each room to every other there were sure to be found
three or four steps either in ascent or descent. Then the
lateral branches were innumerable—inconceivable—and so
returning in upon themselves, that our most exact ideas in
regard to the whole mansion were not very far different from
those with which we pondered upon infinity. During the
five years of my residence here, I was never able to ascertain,
with precision, in what remote locality lay the little sleeping
apartment assigned to myself and some eighteen or twenty
other scholars.

"The schoolroom was the largest in the house—I could
not help thinking, in the world. It was very long, narrow,
and dismally low, with pointed Gothic windows and a ceiling
of oak. In a remote and terror-inspiring angle was a square
enclosure of eight or ten feet, comprising the *sanctum*, 'during
hours,' of our principal, the Reverend Dr. Bransby. It was
a solid structure, with massy door, sooner than open which,
in the absence of the 'Dominie,' we would all have willingly
perished by the *peine forte et dure.* In other angles were two
other similar boxes, far less reverenced, indeed, but still
greatly matters of awe. One of these was the pulpit of the
'classical' usher, one of the 'English and mathematical.'
Interspersed about the room, crossing and recrossing in endless irregularity, were innumerable benches and desks, black,
ancient, and time-worn, piled desperately with much-be-
thumbed books, and so beseamed with initial letters, names
at full length, grotesque figures, and other multiplied efforts
of the knife, as to have entirely lost what little of original

form might have been their portion in days long departed. A huge bucket with water stood at one extremity of the room, and a clock of stupendous dimensions at the other."

" The ardour, the enthusiasm, and the imperiousness," which are declared to have rendered the " William Wilson " of the story a marked character among his schoolmates, so that by slow but natural gradations he obtained an ascendency over all not greatly older than himself, may safely be assumed to represent Poe's own idiosyncrasies, even at this early epoch of his life. A consistency of passion and thought, however diverted or thwarted by occasional circumstance, runs through Poe's whole career, and what was truly representative of him at the first is found a faithful portraiture at the last. " In childhood," he exclaims, " I must have felt with the energy of a man what I now find stamped upon memory in lines as vivid, as deep, and as durable, as the exergues of the Carthaginian medals."

The lad was recalled to America in 1821, and for some months spent his time in what he termed "mere idleness," but which really consisted in composing verses, and in thinking out future poems. Indeed, as he subsequently states, in the interesting *Preface* to his first printed book, its contents were written during the years 1821-22, and before the author had completed his fourteenth year.

# CHAPTER III.

## *BOYHOOD.*

In 1822 Mr. Allan placed his adopted son, who now reassumed his own surname of Poe, in an academy in Richmond, Virginia, in which city the Allans continued to reside. Many most interesting reminiscences of the embryo poet during his attendance at this preparatory school, then kept by Mr. John Clarke, have been placed at our disposal by fellow pupils of Poe, and the following, from the pen of Colonel John T. L. Preston, husband of Mrs. Margaret J. Preston, the poetess, cannot fail to charm :—

"Although I was several years Poe's junior, we sat together at the same form for a year or more at a classical school in Richmond, Virginia. Our master was John Clarke, of Trinity College, Dublin. At that time his school was the one of highest repute in the metropolis. Master Clarke was a hot-tempered, pedantic, bachelor Irishman; but a Latinist of the first order, according to the style of scholarship of that date, he unquestionably was. I have often heard my mother amuse herself by repeating his pompous assurance that in his school her boy should be taught 'only the pure Latinity of the Augustan age.' It is due to his memory * to say, that if her

---

* Professor John Clarke is still alive.—J. H. I.

boy was not properly grounded in his rudiments, it was not the fault of his teacher. What else we were taught I have forgotten; but my drilling in Latin, even to its minutiæ, is clear to my view as if lying on the surface of yesterday.

"Edgar Poe might have been at this time fifteen or sixteen, he being one of the oldest boys in the school, and I one of the youngest. His power and accomplishments captivated me, and something in me, or in him, made him take a fancy to me. In the simple school athletics of those days, when a gymnasium had not been heard of, he was *facile princeps*. He was a swift runner, a wonderful leaper, and what was more rare, a boxer, with some slight training. I remember, too, that he would allow the strongest boy in the school to strike him with full force in the chest. He taught me the secret, and I imitated him, after my measure. It was to inflate the lungs to the uttermost, and at the moment of receiving the blow to exhale the air. It looked surprising, and was, indeed, a little rough; but with a good breast-bone, and some resolution, it was not difficult to stand it. For swimming he was noted, being in many of his athletic proclivities surprisingly like Byron in his youth. There was no one among the schoolboys who would so dare in the midst of the rapids of the James River. I recall one of his races. A challenge to a foot-race had been passed between the two classical schools of the city: we selected Poe as our champion. The race came off one bright May morning at sunrise, in the Capitol Square. Historical truth compels me to add that on this occasion our school was beaten, and we had to pay up our small bets. Poe ran well, but his competitor was a long-legged, Indian-looking fellow, who would have outstripped Atalanta without the help of the golden apples. Ah, how many of those young racers on Capitol

Square that fair May morning, and how many of the crowd that so eagerly looked on, are very still now !

" In our Latin exercises in school Poe was among the first —not first without dispute. We had competitors who fairly disputed the palm. Especially one — Nat Howard — afterwards known as one of the ripest scholars in Virginia, and distinguished also as a profound lawyer. If Howard was less brilliant than Poe, he was far more studious ; for even then the germs of waywardness were developing in the nascent poet, and even then no inconsiderable portion of his time was given to versifying. But if I put Howard as a Latinist on a level with Poe, I do him full justice. One exercise of the school was a favourite one with Poe : it was what was called 'capping verses.' The practice is so absolutely obsolete now, at least in our country, that the term may require explanation.

" Before the close of the school, all the Latinists, without regard to age or respective advancement in the language, were drawn up in a line for ' capping verses ; ' just as, in old-fashioned schools, all scholars had to take their place in the spelling-line before dismission. At the head of the line stood the best scholar, who gave from memory some verse of Latin poetry to be 'capped :' that is, he challenged all the line to give from memory another verse beginning with the same letter. Whoever was able to do this, took the place of the leader ; and in his turn propounded another verse to be capped in like manner. This we called ' simple capping.' ' Double capping ' was more difficult, inasmuch as the responding verse must both begin and end with the same letters as the propounded verse. To give an example, and at the same time to illustrate how a memory, like a sieve, may let through what is valuable, and yet retain in its reticulations a worthless speck, I recall a 'capping' which, while I have forgotten ten thousand things that would have been serviceable if remembered, comes back to me with distinctness after the lapse of so many years.

"Nat Howard stood at the head of the line, and gave out for double capping a verse beginning with *d*, and ending with *m*. It passed Edgar Poe, it passed other good scholars, as well it might, until it reached me, a tyro, away down the line. To the surprise of everybody, and not less to my own, there popped into my mind the line of Virgil :—

> ' *Ducite ab urbe domum, mea carmina, ducite Daphnim.*'

And with pride and amazement I saw myself where I never was before and never was afterwards,—above Nat Howard and Edgar Poe.

"The practice looks absurd, and so it would be now. True, it stored the memory with many good quotations for ready use. But after the fashion of Master Clark—a fashion brought from Trinity—this 'capping verses' was much in vogue, and Edgar Poe was an expert at it.

"He was very fond of the Odes of Horace, and repeated them so often in my hearing that I learned by sound the words of many, before I understood their meaning. In the lilting rhythm of the Sapphics and Iambics, his ear, as yet untutored in more complicated harmonies, took special delight. Two odes, in particular, have been humming in my ear all my life since, set to the tune of his recitation :—

> ' Jam satis terris nivis atque diræ
> Grandinis misit Pater, et rubente '—

and,

> ' Non ebur neque aureum
> Mea renidet in domo lacunar,' &c.

"When I think of his boyhood, his career, and his fate, the poet, whose lines I first learned from his musical lips, supplies me with his epitaph :

> ' Ille, mordaci velut icta ferro
> Pinus, aut impulsa cupressus Euro,
> Procidit late, posuitque collum in
> Pulvere Teucro.'

"I remember that Poe was also a very fine French scholar. Yet, with all his superiorities, he was not the master-spirit, nor even the favourite, of the school. I assign, from my recollection, this place to Howard. Poe, as I recall my impressions now, was self-willed, capricious, inclined to be imperious, and though of generous impulses, not steadily kind, or even amiable ; and so what he would exact was refused to him. I add another thing which had its influence, I am sure.

"At the time of which I speak, Richmond was one of the most aristocratic cities on this side the Atlantic. I hasten to say that this is not so now. Aristocracy, like capping verses, has fallen into desuetude—perhaps for the same reason : times having changed, other things pay better. Richmond was certainly then very English, and very aristocratic. A school is, of its nature, democratic ; but still boys will unconsciously bear about the odour of their fathers' notions, good or bad. Of Edgar Poe it was known that his parents had been players, and that he was dependent upon the bounty that is bestowed upon an adopted son. All this had the effect of making the boys decline his leadership ; and on looking back on it since, I fancy it gave him a fierceness he would otherwise not have had. . . .

"Not a little of Poe's time in school, and out of it, was

occupied with writing verses. As we sat together, he would show them to me, and even sometimes ask my opinion, and now and then my assistance. I recall at this moment his consulting me about one particular line, as to whether the word 'groat' would properly rhyme with 'not.' It would not surprise me now if I should be able, by looking over his juvenile poems, to identify that very line. As it is my only chance for poetic fame, I must, I think, undertake the search.

"My boyish admiration was so great for my schoolfellow's genius, that I requested his permission to carry his portfolio home for the inspection of my mother. If her enthusiasm was less than mine, her judgment did not hesitate to praise the verses very highly ; and her criticism might well gratify the boyish poet ; for she was a lady who to a natural love for literature, inherited from her father, Edmund Randolph,* had added the most thorough and careful culture obtained by the most extensive reading of the English classics,—the established mode of female education in those days. Here, then, you have the first critic to whom were submitted the verses of our world-famed poet. Her warm appreciation of the boy's genius and work was proof of her own critical taste."

One paragraph of Colonel Preston's recollections throws a lurid and most suggestive light upon the causes which rendered the boy's early life unhappy, and tended to blight his budding hopes. Although, as seen, mixing with scions of the best families, and endowed with the innate pride derivable from gentle

* The well-known statesman.—J. H. I.

birth—fostered by all the indulgences of wealth and
the consciousness of intellect—Edgar Poe was made
to feel that his parentage was obscure, and his position
in society dependent upon the charitable caprice of a
benefactor.  Many boys might have endured such a
condition of life with equanimity, but to one of this
lad's temperament it must have been a source of continual torment, and all allusions to it gall and worm-
wood for his haughty spirit.  Generally, Mr. Allan
appears to have been proud of his handsome and precocious godson, and willing enough to provide him
with the advantages proffered by educational institu-
tions; but of parental affection, and of that family
sympathy for which the poor orphan boy yearned—
as his words and works prove—he seems to have been
utterly devoid.  Not but what the imperious youth
was frequently indulged in all money could purchase,
yet the pettings and rebuffs which he was alternately
subjected to were scarcely calculated to conciliate *his*
disposition.  Throughout life a morbid sensitiveness
to affection was one of Poe's most distinguishing traits,
and it was the want of this which drove him frequently
to seek in the society of dumb creatures the love
denied him, or which he sometimes *believed* denied
him, by human beings.  In his terrible tale of *The
Black Cat* there is a paragraph which those who were
intimately acquainted with its author will at once

recognise the autobiographical fidelity of. "From my infancy," remarks Poe, "I was noted for the docility and humanity of my disposition. My tenderness of heart was even so conspicuous as to make me the jest of my companions. I was especially fond of animals, and was indulged by my parents with a great variety of pets. With these I spent most of my time, and never was so happy as when feeding and caressing them. This peculiarity of character grew with my growth, and in my manhood I derived from it one of my principal sources of pleasure. To those who have cherished an affection for a faithful and sagacious dog, I need hardly be at the trouble of explaining the nature or the intensity of the gratification thus derivable. There is something in the unselfish and self-sacrificing love of a brute, which goes directly to the heart of him who has had frequent occasion to test the paltry friendship and gossamer fidelity of mere *man*."

Many of Poe's schoolfellows at the Richmond Academy corroborate and supplement Colonel Preston's reminiscences. Dr. R. C. Ambler writes : " I recollect my old playmate Edgar Allan Poe. I passed my early life in the city of Richmond, and in the years 1823-24 I was in the habit of constant intercourse with the boy. No one now living, I dare say, had better opportunities of becoming acquainted with his physique, as for two summers we stripped together for a bath daily, and learned to swim in the same pool in Shockoe Creek. . . . Poe was not apt at learning to swim, though at a subsequent period he became famous for swimming from Mayo's Bridge to Warwick." In allusion to this long remembered boyish feat, the poet himself remarked, " Any ' swimmer in the falls ' in my days would have swum the Hellespont, and thought nothing of the matter. I swam from Ludlam's Wharf to Warwick (six miles) in a hot June sun, against one of the strongest tides ever known in the river. It would have been a feat comparatively easy to swim twenty miles in still water. I would not think much," concluded Poe, in his strain of not infrequent exaggeration, " of attempting to swim the British Channel from Dover to Calais." Whatever he might not think much of " attempting," the lad did not, certainly, shrink from doing a deed of no little daring in his famous swim, an account of which is thus furnished by Colonel Robert Mayo, junior, at that time a companion and schoolmate of the poet :—" I started with Poe in his celebrated swim from Richmond to Warwick Bar, six miles down James River. The day was oppressively hot, and I concluded rather than endure the infliction to stop at Tree Hill, three miles from town. Poe, however, braved the sun and kept on, reaching the goal, but emerging from the water with neck, face, and back blistered."

The truth of this feat having been publicly questioned, Poe, who was intolerant of contradiction, obtained from Dr. Cabell and published the following certification of his prowess :—

"I was one of several who witnessed this swimming feat. We accompanied Mr. Poe in boats. Messrs. Robert Stannard, John Lyle (since dead), Robert Saunders, John Munford, I think, and one or two others, were also of the party. Mr. Poe did not seem at all fatigued, and *walked* back to Richmond immediately after the feat—which was undertaken for a wager. ROBERT G. CABELL."

A yet more dangerous exploit in natation is recorded of the daring boy by Colonel Mayo. One day in midwinter, when standing on the banks of the James River, Poe bantered his companion into jumping in, in order to swim to a certain point with him. After floundering about in the nearly frozen stream for some time they reached the piles upon which Mayo's Bridge then rested, and were glad enough to stop and try to gain the shore by climbing up the log abutment to the bridge. To their dismay, upon reaching the bridge, they discovered that its flooring overlapped the abutment by several feet, and that ascent by such means was impossible. Nothing remained for them but to descend and retrace their steps, which, weary and partly frozen, they did: Poe reached the land in an exhausted state, whilst Mayo was fished out by a friendly boat,

just as he was about to succumb.   On getting ashore,
Poe was seized with a violent attack of vomiting, and
both the lads were ill for several weeks.   Colonel Mayo
recalls Poe to mind as a haughty, handsome, impetuous
boy, self-willed, defiant, and not indisposed for fight,
but with great mental power and an ever-present
anxiety to grapple with and solve difficult mental
problems.

Dr. Ambler, recurring to this period of Poe's career,
remarks, " Of course I was too young at that date to
appreciate the poet's mental capabilities; but I remember to have heard some verses of his, in the shape of a
satire upon the members of a debating society to which
he belonged. . . I cannot recall a line of these verses,
but do remember that I envied him his ability to write
them.   These lines, as far as I know, were never published, but were circulated in manuscript among the
boys, and were, probably, the first known out of his
family."

Mr. John Clarke having relinquished the guidance
of the Richmond school was succeeded, in the autumn
of 1823, by a Mr. William Burke, and amongst the
pupils who remained in his charge was Edgar Allan
Poe.   Mr. Andrew Johnston, another of his schoolfellows at Richmond, states that when he went to
Mr. Burke's, on the 1st of October 1823, he found
Poe there.   " I knew him before," he writes, " but not

well, there being two, if not three, years difference in our ages. We went to school together all through 1824, and the early part of 1825. Some time in the latter year (I cannot recollect at what time exactly) he left the school. . . Poe was a much more advanced scholar than any of us ; but there was no other class for him—that being the highest—and he had nothing to do, or but little, to keep his headship of the class. I dare say he liked it well, for he was fond of desultory reading, and even then wrote verses. . . We all recognised and admired his great and varied talents, and were proud of him as the most distinguished schoolboy of the town. At that time Poe was slight in person and figure, but well made, active, sinewy, and graceful. In athletic exercises he was foremost. Especially, he was the best, the most daring, and most enduring swimmer that I ever saw in the water. . . . His disposition was amiable, and his manners pleasant and courteous." *

These somewhat similarly minded reminiscences by the poet's playmates—doubtless slightly, albeit unconsciously, biassed in tone by the after celebrity of Poe—serve to illustrate and prove that even at that early age the lad had strongly impressed his comrades with a belief in his intellectual superiority, and that he had already begun to entertain a proud and somewhat

* Didier, *Life of Edgar A. Poe,* pp. 33, 34.

pugnacious contempt for those less richly endowed by
nature. Other equally marked idiosyncrasies of his
character — extraordinary fidelity of friendship, and
intense sensitiveness to kindness—are strikingly portrayed by some well-authenticated incidents in this
period of his life, and to which the late Mrs. Whitman
was the first to draw attention.* The correctness of
her remarks in connection with these episodes have
been amply confirmed by the correspondence of Mrs.
Clemm and Poe himself. Referring to the passionate,
almost fanatical, devotion of the poet for those who
became the objects of his affection, Mrs. Whitman
relates this characteristic anecdote of his boyhood :—

"While at the academy in Richmond, he one day
accompanied a schoolmate to his home, where he saw
for the first time Mrs. H[elen] S[tannard], the mother
of his young friend. This lady, on entering the room,
took his hand and spoke some gentle and gracious
words of welcome, which so penetrated the sensitive
heart of the orphan boy as to deprive him of the
power of speech, and for a time almost of consciousness itself. He returned home in a dream, with but
one thought, one hope in life—to hear again the sweet
and gracious words that had made the desolate world
so beautiful to him, and filled his lonely heart with

* *Edgar Poe and his Critics,* pp. 48-55.

the oppression of a new joy. This lady afterwards became the confidant of all his boyish sorrows, and hers was the one redeeming influence that saved and guided him in the earlier days of his turbulent and passionate youth."

Writing on this same subject, Mrs. Clemm records that he entertained a most profound devotion for this lady, and that "when he was unhappy at home (which was very often the case), he went to her for sympathy, for consolation, and for advice." But, alas! the sad destiny which appeared to haunt the poor lad, and all dear to him, overtook his beloved friend! This lady herself was overwhelmed by fearful and peculiar sorrows, and at the very moment when her guiding voice was most needed, fell a prey to mental aliena-tion, and when she died and was entombed in a neighbouring cemetery, her poor boyish admirer could not endure the thought of her lying there lonely and forsaken in her vaulted home. For months after her decease, Poe—like his great Hungarian contemporary Petöfi, at the grave of his girl-love Etelka—would go nightly to visit the tomb of his revered friend, and when the nights were very drear and cold, "when the autumnal rains fell, and the winds wailed mourn-fully over the graves, he lingered longest, and came away most regretfully."

For years, if not for life, the memory of this

unfortunate lady tinged all Poe's fancies, and filled
his mind with saddening things.   In a letter, written
within a twelvemonth of his own death, to Mrs.
Whitman, the poet broke through his usual reticence
as to the facts of his early life, and confessed that his
exquisitely beautiful stanzas " To Helen," * were inspired by the memory of this lady—by " the one
idolatrous and purely ideal love" of his tempest-tossed
boyhood.   In the early versions of his youthful verses,
the name of " Helen " continually recurs, and it was
undoubtedly to her that he devoted "The Pæan," a
juvenile poem which subsequently he greatly improved
in both rhythm and form, and republished under the
musical name of " Lenore."   The weird thoughts
which he experienced when he beheld this lady
robed in her grave garments are hinted at in
" Irene," † and the description which he gave to a
friend of the fantasies that haunted his brain during
his desolate vigils in the cemetery,—the nameless
fears and indescribable phantasmata—

> " Flapping from out their Condor wings
> Invisible Woe ! "—

she compares to those which overwhelmed De
Quincey at the burial of his sweet sister-playmate.
   Those willing to study Poe's idiosyncrasies should

* Beginning, " Helen, thy beauty is to me."
† Published in 1831.

not object to linger over this little-known epoch of
his story, because we are indeed convinced that in
"those solitary churchyard vigils, with all their
associated memories," Mrs. Whitman has found "a
key to much that seems strange and abnormal in the
poet's after life." There can be no doubt that those
who would seek the clue to the psychological phenomena of his strange existence—"that intellect," as
Poe himself remarked, which would try to reduce
his "phantasm to the commonplace"—must know,
and even analyse this phase of his being. The mind
which could so steadfastly trace, step by step, the
gruesome gradations of *sentience after death*, as does
Edgar Poe in his weird "Colloquy of Monos and
Una," must indeed have been one that had frequently
sought to wrest its earthy secrets from the charnel
house.

Throughout life Poe was haunted by the idea that
the dead are not wholly dead to consciousness—was
haunted, as Mrs. Whitman says, "by ideas of terror and
indescribable awe, at the thought of that mysterious
waking sleep, that powerless and dim vitality, in
which 'the dead' are presumed, according to our
popular theology, to await 'the general resurrection
at the last day'"—and it was this feeling, those who
knew him believe, that restrained him more than once
from contracting another marriage after his beloved

wife's death. The feeling, so powerfully expounded
in some of his tales and his poems *—

> " *Lest the dead, who is forsaken,*
> *May not be happy now,*"—

overclouded his mind until the very last days of his
" lonesome latter years."

* Compare " Eleonora ; " " The Bridal Ballad ; " and article " Un-
dine," in *Marginalia.*

## CHAPTER IV.

*FIRST LOVE.*

BETWEEN the date of Poe's leaving Mr. Burke's school
and his departure for the University of Virginia, early
in the following year, 1826, little or nothing authentic
is known of the youthful poet's deeds or adventures.
During this interregnum of six months or so, there is
good reason for believing, however, that he was plea-
santly engaged in both making verses and making
love, a combination of occupations, it need scarcely
be pointed out, by no means unfrequent.

Quoting the assertion of " George Sand " that " *les
anges ne sont plus pures que le cœur d'un jeune homme
qui aime en vérité*," Poe remarks that " the hyperbole
is scarcely less than true," but that " it would be truth
itself were it averred of the love of him who is at the
same time young and a poet. The boyish poet-love,"
he emphatically declares, " is indisputably that one of
the human sentiments which most nearly realises our
dreams of the chastened voluptuousness of heaven."
Thinking and speaking thus, and having in memory a

similar influence exercised over a short period of his
earlier life, he refers to the boyish poet-love of Byron
for Mary Chaworth, as an earnest and long-abiding
attachment that sublimated and purified from earthli-
ness all his works alluding to it.   And yet, he adds,
this passion, " if passion it can properly be termed,
was of the most thoroughly romantic, shadowy, and
imaginative character.   It was born of the hour, and
of the youthful necessity to love. . . . It had no
peculiar regard to the person, or to the character, or to
the reciprocating affection of Mary Chaworth.   Any
maiden, not immediately and positively repulsive,"
he deems Byron would have loved in similar circumstances of frequent and unrestricted intercourse, such
as the children are represented as having enjoyed.
" The result," opines Poe, " was not merely natural,
or merely probable, it was as inevitable as destiny
itself."

Any ordinary maiden would have served "sufficiently well as the incarnation of the ideal that haunted
the fancy of the poet," continues the young critic, notwithstanding the fact that the affection may not have
been reciprocated ; or, " if *she* felt at all, it was only
while the magnetism of *his* actual presence compelled
her to feel."   With evident remembrance of the ideal
of his own boyhood before him, he believes that to
Mary Chaworth Byron was merely " a not unhand-

some, and not ignoble, but somewhat portionless, somewhat eccentric young man," whilst "she to him was
the Egeria of his dreams—the Venus Aphrodite that
sprang, in full and supernal loveliness, from the bright
foam upon the storm-tormented ocean of his thoughts."
Reading his own story by these words, it is suggestive
to find how closely the loves of the two contemporary
poets were paralleled.

Between the years 1822–25, as has been told,
Edgar Poe was a scholar in a well-known academy at
Richmond. The adopted son and reputed heir of Mr.
Allan, and "a not unhandsome," if "somewhat eccentric young man," the youthful poet made no mean
figure among his Virginian companions, notwithstanding any drawbacks incidental to his obscure parentage.
Admired by his fellow-students for his superior educational attainments, his daring athletic feats, and for
a certain magnetic rather than sympathetic influence
which he exercised over them, it is not surprising to
learn that he was introduced into, and mingled with,
the best society of the Old Dominion. In the
coteries into which he was received was a little
maiden but a year or two younger than himself, who
speedily became fascinated by the charms of his
presence.

S. Elmira Royster lived with her father opposite to
the Allans in Richmond, and in the usual course of

events she made the acquaintance of their adopted son. She remembers Edgar Poe as "a beautiful boy," as not very talkative, and whose "general manner was sad," but whose conversation, when he did talk, was truly pleasant. " Of his own parents he never spoke," but " he was devoted to the first Mrs. Allan, and she to him. He had very few associates, but he was very intimate with Ebenezer Berling, a widow's son of about the same age as himself. Berling was an interesting, intelligent young man, but somewhat inclined to dissipation. They used to visit our house together very frequently. Edgar," continues the lady, "was very generous," and " warm and zealous in any cause he was interested in, being enthusiastic and impulsive." Dowered with " the hate of hate, the scorn of scorn," the youthful lover is remembered to have had strong prejudices, and, with his adoration for beauty already fully developed, to have detested everything coarse or wanting in refinement. It is also within the memory of the lady that her young admirer drew beautifully: ".he drew a pencil likeness of me," she relates, " in a few minutes." He was even then passionately fond of music, "an art which in after life he loved so well."

The love passages were kept up between the youthful pair until Poe left for the University ; he had, indeed, engaged to marry Miss Royster, and wrote to her frequently after his departure. Her father intercepted the letters, deeming his daughter "o'er young to marry," and it was not until a year or so later, and when, having attained the mature age of seventeen, she became Mrs. Shelton, that the young poet learned how it was that his passionate appeals had failed to elicit any response from the object of his affections. The influence and memory of this attachment tinged much of Poe's juvenile verse, threading like a misty autobiographic reminiscence through the initial version of his "Tamerlane," and pervading with unpassionate melancholy many of his earliest stanzas. Recurring once more to his remarks on Byron's boy-love, how naturally do these words appear to shadow forth the thoughts appertaining to the result of his own youthful amours. "It is perhaps better," he thinks, "for the mere romance of the love passages between the two, that their intercourse was broken up in early life, and never uninterruptedly resumed in after years. Whatever of warmth, whatever of soul passion, whatever of the truer share and essentiality of romance was elicited during the youthful association, is to be attributed altogether to the poet. If *she* felt at all, it was only while the magnetism of *his* actual presence compelled her to feel. If *she* responded at all, it was merely because the necromancy of *his* words of fire could not do otherwise than extort a response. In

absence, the bard bore easily with him all the fancies
which were the basis of his flame—a flame which
absence itself but served to keep in vigour—while the
less ideal but at the same time the less really sub-
stantial affection of his lady-love, perished utterly and
forthwith, through simple lack of the element which
had fanned it into being."

# CHAPTER V.

## *ALMA MATER.*

THE University of Virginia, or "Jefferson's University," as it has been frequently called in honour of President Jefferson, by whom it was founded, is beautifully situated upon an extensive plateau in the centre of the Old Dominion. It is surrounded by some of the most picturesque scenery in the United States, and in every respect reflects credit upon its worthy and disinterested founder. The establishment of this University was a darling, and indeed a daring, scheme of President Jefferson; and had occupied a very large portion of his time from the first inception of the plan in 1779, until the opening of the institution on March 7th, 1825. The founder's labours in connection with the University were immense, and even after all opposition, latent and declared, had been overcome by the successful completion of the various buildings connected with it; and by the engagement of such men for the professorships as Charles Bonny-castle, the late Thomas Hewitt Key, George Long,

Dunglison, Blättermann, and other well-known men, his difficulties were by no means ended. His idea had been to make the students their own governors, and in lieu of punishments, to rely upon appeals to their honour and patriotism. A code of laws was framed in accordance with these views, but unfortunately proved useless; and the appeals to " their reason, their hopes, and their generous feelings," which the illustrious patriot had so firmly relied upon for swaying the youthful multitude, ended in confusion. This disaster arose, apparently, from a mistaken view the students took of the duties required of them. The librarian, Mr. William Wertenbaker, the only surviving officer of the earliest *régime*, informs us :—

" The session of 1825 was commenced without any discipline at all, and without an effort on the part of the Faculty to enforce obedience to the laws. They were expecting and waiting for the students to inaugurate Mr. Jefferson's system of self-government, but this they resolutely refused to do. Neither the entreaties of Mr. Jefferson, nor the persuasion of the professors, could induce a single student to accept the office of Censor. The plan was that a Board of Censors, consisting of six of the most discreet students, should inquire into the facts in all cases of minor offences, and name the punishment which they thought proportioned to the offence.

" In this state of affairs, and for several months, insubordination, lawlessness, and riot ruled the institution, and became so intolerable to the professors that they suspended operations, and tendered their resignations to the Board of Visitors. The

Board met immediately ; abandoned the plan of self-government ; enacted new laws ; ordered a course of rigid discipline
to be pursued, and invested the Faculty with full authority
to rule and govern the institution.

" In exercising the power now granted them, the Faculty
(as in the circumstances it was quite natural for them to do)
perhaps erred in going to the opposite extreme of punishing
offenders with too great severity. . . At no period during the
past history of the University were the Faculty more diligent
in ferreting out offenders, and more severe in punishing them,
than during the session of 1826. . . .

" Mr. Poe was a student during the second session, which
commenced February 1st, and terminated December 15th,
1826. He signed the matriculation book on the 14th of
February, and remained in good standing until the session
closed. . . . He entered the schools of Ancient and Modern
Languages, attending the lectures on Latin, Greek, French,
Spanish, and Italian. I was a member of the last three classes,
and can testify that he was tolerably regular in his attendance,
and a successful student, having obtained distinction at the
final examination in Latin and French, and this was at that
time the highest honour a student could obtain. The present
regulations in regard to degrees had not then been adopted.
Under existing regulations, he would have graduated in
the two languages above-named, and have been entitled to
diplomas."

Dr. Harrison, Chairman of the Faculty, fully confirms
this statement of Poe's classmate, stating that the poet
was a great favourite among his fellow-students at
Charlottesville, and that he is remembered for the
remarkable rapidity with which he prepared his recita-

tions, and their general accuracy ; his translations from the living languages being especially noteworthy.

Many of his classmates still retain a vivid recollection of their gifted companion, not from the fact of any particular geniality or *bonhomie* on his part, for he was always of a wayward and exclusive disposition, but from his self-reliant pride, and from the indisputable fact that he was *facile princeps* in nearly all their pursuits, mental and physical. Mr. John Willis, a fellow-student at the University,* recalls Poe as one who "had many noble qualities," and whom nature had endowed "with more of genius, and a far greater diversity of talent, than any other whom it had been my lot to have known," but, adds this gentleman, "his disposition was rather *retiring*, and he had few intimate associates."

This reserve of Poe is noticed and confirmed by many others who came in general contact with him. Mr. Thomas Bolling, another of his fellow-students, says, "I was *acquainted* with him in his youthful days, but that was about all. My impression was, and is, that no one could say that he *knew* him. He wore a melancholy face always, and even his smile—for I do not ever remember to have seen him laugh—seemed to be forced. When he engaged sometimes with others in athletic exercises, in which, so far as high or long

* In a letter to the late Mrs. Whitman.

jumping, I believe he excelled all the rest, Poe, with the same ever sad face, appeared to participate in what was amusement to the others, more as a task than sport. Upon one occasion, upon a slight declivity, he ran and jumped twenty feet, which was more than the others could do, although some attained nineteen feet. His chief competitor in these exercises was Labranche, an especial friend of mine from Louisiana, who, although of lower stature by several inches, had had the advantage, previous to entering the University, of being educated in France, where gymnastics are taught and practised as part of the course." Powell, in his *Authors of America*, alludes to Poe having had the habit of covering the walls of his dormitory with charcoal sketches; Mr. John Willis states that he had a talent for drawing, and that the walls of his room at college were completely covered with his crayon sketches, whilst Mr. Bolling mentions in connection with his artistic facility the following suggestive incidents. The two young men invested in Byron's Poems, purchasing copies of an English edition that contained several handsome steel engravings. Poe appeared much interested in these plates, and upon visiting him a few days later, Mr. Bolling found him engaged in copying one with crayon on the ceiling of his dormitory. He continued to amuse himself in this way from time to time, says our authority, until he had filled all the space in his

room. These life-size figures were, in the memory of
those who saw them, extremely ornamental and attrac-
tive, but all such vestiges of his boyish aspirations
have long since disappeared. Mr. Bolling remarks
that he never saw Poe attempt to sketch anything on
paper, as if, indeed, such material afforded too limited
a space for the boundless fancies of his youthful
ambition.

Mr. Bolling remembers that when he was talking
to his eccentric associate, Poe continued to scratch
away with his pencil as if writing, and when his visitor
jestingly remarked on his want of politeness, he
answered that he had been all attention, and proved
that he had by suitable comment, giving as a reason
for his apparent want of courtesy that he was trying
to *divide his mind*—carry on a conversation, and at
the same time write sense on a totally different subject! Several times did Mr. Bolling detect him
engaged in these attempts at mental division; and he
says the verses handed to him as the part results of
the dual labours certainly rhymed pretty well.
Whether this reminiscence only affords an early
instance of Poe's inveterate love of quizzical mystification, or, as is more probable, of his attempts at mental
analysis, it is wonderfully suggestive of the later
man.

Powell records that the poet's time at the University

was divided between lectures, debating societies, and rambles in the Blue Ridge mountains, and of this last-named occupation—so congenial to one who shrank from contact with unsympathising or uncomprehending companions—Poe has left some vivid reminiscences in various parts of his works. Alone, or accompanied only by a dog, he was in the habit of making long expeditions into what he deemed the " wild and dreary hills that lie westward and southward of Charlottesville, and are there dignified by the title of the Ragged Mountains." Alluding to a solitary ramble through the unfrequented fastnesses of this chain of lofty hills, he indulges in the following train of ideas, so accordant with his theories of thought: —" The scenery which presented itself on all sides, although scarcely entitled to be called grand, had about it an indescribable and, to me, a delicious aspect of dreary desolation. The solitude seemed absolutely virgin. I could not help believing that the green sods and the gray rocks upon which I trod had been trodden never before by the foot of a human being. So entirely secluded, and in fact inaccessible, except through a series of accidents, is the entrance of the ravine, that it is by no means impossible that I was indeed the first adventurer—the very first and sole adventurer who had ever penetrated its recesses."

But these lonely rambles and their attendant day-dreams were the occasional relaxations of a hard-working student; among the professors he had the reputation of being a sober, quiet, orderly young man, and the officials of the University bear witness to the fact that his behaviour was uniformly that of an intelligent and polished gentleman.  In evidence of his generally studious conduct Mr. Wertenbaker records that, " on one occasion Professor Blättermann requested his Italian class to render into English verse a portion of the lesson in Tasso, which he had assigned them for the next lecture.  He did not require this of them as a regular class exercise, but recommended it as one from which he thought the student would derive benefit.  At the next lecture on Italian, the professor stated from his chair that ' Mr. Poe was the only member of the class who had responded to his suggestion,' and paid a very high compliment to his performance."

Referring to his own personal experience of the youthful poet, Mr. Wertenbaker says, " As librarian I had frequent official intercourse with Mr. Poe, but it was at or near the close of the Session before I met him in the social circle.  After spending an evening together at a private house, he invited me, on our return, into his room.  It was a cold night in December, and his fire having gone pretty nearly out, by the aid of some tallow candles, and the fragments of a small table which he broke up for the purpose, he soon rekindled it, and by its comfortable blaze I spent a very pleasant hour with him. On this occasion he spoke with regret of the large amount of money he had wasted, and of the debts he had contracted, during the session. If my memory be not at fault, he estimated his indebtedness at $2000, and though they were gaming debts, he was earnest and emphatic in the declaration that he was bound by honour to pay them at the earliest opportunity." Whilst at the University, Poe appears to have been much addicted to gambling, seeking, in the temporary excitement and absorbing nature of cards, that refuge from sorrowful thought which he subsequently sought for in other sources. Although his practice of gaming did escape detection, Mr. Wertenbaker assures us that " the hardihood, intemperance, and reckless wildness imputed to him by biographers—had he been guilty of them—must inevitably have come to the knowledge of the Faculty, and met with merited punishment. The records," he continues, " of which I was then, and am still, the custodian, attest that at no time during the Session did he fall under the censure of the Faculty." Although Poe may, and doubtless did, occasionally take his share in a college frolic, Mr. Wertenbaker most emphatically repudiates the assertion that he was habitually intemperate, adding, " I often saw him in the lecture room and in the library, but never in the slightest degree under the influence of intoxicating liquors."

"Poe's connection with the University was dissolved by the termination of the session, on the 15th of December 1826, when he wanted little more than a month to attain the age of eighteen. The date of his birth was plainly entered in his own handwriting on the matriculation book. . . He never returned to the University, and I think it probable that the night I visited him was the last he spent here," says our informant, drawing this inference from the fact that, having no further need of his candles and table, the poet used them for fuel.

As an interesting and suggestive memento of Poe's residence at Charlottesville, Mr. Wertenbaker has furnished us with a copy, from the register, of a list of books the poet borrowed from the library whilst a student; and those who have studied his works will recognise the good use made, in after life, of the young collegian's selection. Rollin's "Histoire Ancienne," "Histoire Romaine," Robertson's "America," Marshall's "Washington," Voltaire's "Histoire Particulière," and Dufief's "Nature Displayed," are the works he made use of.

Short as was Edgar Poe's University career, he left such honourable memories behind him, that his *alma mater* has been only too proud to enrol his name among her sons. His adopted father, however, does not appear to have regarded his godson's collegiate proceedings with equal favour; whatever view he may have taken of the lad's scholastic successes, he resolutely refused to liquidate his gambling debts—his debts of *honour*—and the consequence was a violent altercation, terminating in the young student hastily quitting his home, with the determination of trusting to his own resources to make his way in the world. For a time he appears to have thought of supporting himself by literature, and, like most neophytes in that career, commenced with a volume of verse. Additional motive for his hasty departure from Richmond may be found in the fact of Miss Royster's marriage to Mr. Shelton, an event doubtless commemorated in some lines " To ———," included in his first—the 1827 —volume, beginning

> " I saw thee on the bridal day,
>     When a burning blush came o'er thee ;
> Though happiness around thee lay,
>     The world all love before thee."

It may well be conjectured that a youth of Poe's proud and impetuous disposition would scarcely remain plodding quietly at home, constantly in sight of another enjoying happiness which he had, presumedly, lost.

## CHAPTER VI.

*DAWNINGS OF GENIUS.*

EDGAR POE'S first literary venture was printed in its author's natal city of Boston, in 1827. What caused him to visit his birthplace is a mystery. Whether a longing to learn something further of his mother and her family—and neglected honours to her memory caused him frequent qualms of conscience in after years—or whether he merely pilgrimaged to the capital of Massachusetts in hopes of there finding a good market for his poetic labours, has not been, and probably never will be, discovered. At all events, the remembrances which he brought away with him of the " American Athens " were anything but pleasing, although then and there it was, apparently, that he made the acquaintance of his mother's friends, the Ushers and the Wilsons, people whose names, at least, he made literary use of a few years later on.

His first known literary venture, a tiny tome consisting of only forty pages, inclusive of *Preface* and *Notes*, although printed for publication, was " suppressed through circumstances of a private nature." The title of the little book runs thus :—

## TAMERLANE

### AND

## OTHER POEMS.

#### BY A BOSTONIAN.

" Young heads are giddy, and young hearts are warm,
And make mistakes for manhood to reform."—*Cowper.*

BOSTON : CALVIN S. THOMAS.

1827.

What the private reasons were which caused the suppression of this most interesting memento of the poet's early life can only be conjectured. It is not improbable that the too palpable nature of the autobiographical allusions, the doubtless obnoxious family researches which might be instituted by some, when the " Bostonian " of the title-page became identified with Edgar Allan Poe, and perchance the appeal for forgiveness foreshadowed in the motto from Cowper, all combined, or any one separately, may have led to the withdrawal of the book from circulation.

In the *Preface* to this volume the youthful poet informs his anticipated readers, that the greater part of its contents " were written in the year 1821–22, when the author had not completed his fourteenth year. They were, of course, not intended for publication," he

remarks, and " why they are now published concerns
no one but himself.   Of the smaller pieces," he deems
" very little need be said : they, perhaps, savour too
much of egotism, but they were written by one too
young to have any knowledge of the world but from
his own breast.   In ' Tamerlane,' " says the boy-poet,
" he has endeavoured to expose the folly of even *risking*
the best feelings of the heart at the shrine of Ambition.
He is conscious that in this there are many faults
(besides that of the general character of the poem)
which, he flatters himself, he could with little trouble
have corrected, but, unlike many of his predecessors,
has been too fond of his early productions to amend
them in his *old age.*   He will not," he confesses, " say
that he is indifferent as to the success of these poems
—it might stimulate him to other attempts—but he
can safely assert that failure will not at all influence
him in a resolution already adopted.   This is challeng-
ing criticism—let it be so.   *Nos hæc novimus esse nihil,"*
which concluding assertion, it may be remarked, he
lived to prove the falsity of.

Following the preface is " Tamerlane," which occupies
about seventeen pages of the booklet ; it is a very
different poem from that of Poe's later years, known
by the same title, and is replete with the Byronian
influence.   A more connected story is afforded by this
version than by the later editions ; the heroine is

named as Ada, and the hero as Alexis, "Tamerlane" being deemed to have been only a *nom-de-guerre* of the famous warrior. Very many lines, indeed many whole stanzas, are filled with personal allusions to their author, as those alluding to his innate pride and habitual day-dreaming, and when referring to one loved and lost even before what *passion* was could be known. A belief in his own budding powers is certainly portrayed in such lines as—

> "The soul which feels its innate right—
> The mystic empire and high power
> Given by the energetic might
> Of genius, at its natal hour "—

and

> " There is a power in the high spirit
> To *know* the fate it will inherit :
> The soul, which knows such power, will still
> Find *pride* the ruler of its will "—

and allusion to those around him may readily be discovered in those sceptics

> " Who hardly will conceive
> That any should become 'great,' born
> In their own sphere—will not believe
> That they shall stoop in life to one
> Whom daily they are wont to see
> Familiarly—whom Fortune's sun
> Hath ne'er shone dazzlingly upon,
> Lowly—and of their own degree."

The idea which the young aspirant for fame enunciated in verse, he also devoted a note to, to demonstrate that it is very difficult " to make the generality of mankind believe that one with whom they are upon terms of intimacy shall be called in the world a 'great man,'" and he deems the evident reason to be that " there are few great men, and that their actions are constantly viewed by the mass of people through the medium of distance.   The prominent parts of their characters are alone noted ; and those properties which are minute and common to every one, not being observed, seem to have no connection with a great character."

The " Fugitive Pieces " which follow " Tamerlane " are all more or less tinged with the same cast of thought which from first to last characterised their author, although perhaps more indicative of the influence of contemporary poets than any of his later productions.   Haunting sorrow, strong ambition, and mental rambles into the shadowy realms of dreamland, permeate these earliest verses of his boyhood as profusely as they do the musical refrains of his " lonesome latter years."   In one of these mental adumbrations he cries—

"Oh! that my young life were a lasting dream !
   My spirit not awaking till the beam
   Of an eternity should bring the morrow.
   Yes ! though that long dream were of hopeless sorrow,

> 'Twere better than the cold reality
> Of waking life, to him whose heart must be,
> And hath been, still upon the lovely earth,
> A chaos of deep passion from his birth."

The "Visit of the Dead," which follows the piece quoted from, is evidently inspired by Byron's "Dream," whilst a succeeding lyric from the same source is confessedly entitled "Imitation;" some lines in it, however, are very characteristic, such as—

> "A dark unfathomed tide
> Of interminable pride—
> A mystery and a dream
> Should my early life seem."

The well-known little lyric, "A Dream," which appeared in this edition, also contained this initial stanza —afterwards omitted—of significant self-allusion :—

> "A wildered being from my birth,
> My spirit spurned control;
> But now, abroad on the wide earth,
> Where wanderest thou, my soul?"

whilst the following penultimate piece, entitled "The Happiest Day," to those who have thus far followed his story, cannot fail to be replete with autobiographical implication :—

> "The happiest day—the happiest hour—
> My seared and blighted heart hath known;
> The highest hope of pride and power,
> I feel hath flown.

"Of power ! said I ?  Yes ! such I ween ;
 But they have vanished long, alas !
The visions of my youth have been—
 But let them pass.

" And pride, what have I now with thee ?
 Another brow may ev'n inherit
The venom thou hast poured on me—
 Be still, my spirit.

" The happiest day—the happiest hour—
 Mine eyes shall see—have ever seen ;
The brightest glance of pride and power,
 I feel—have been.

" But were that hope of pride and power
 Now offered with the pain
Ev'n *then* I felt—that brightest hour
 I would not live again :

" For on its wing was dark alloy,
 And as it fluttered, fell
An essence, powerful to destroy
 A soul that knew it well."

With the lines entitled "The Lake"—the best poem in the collection—Edgar Poe's earliest literary venture closes.

Taken altogether, and due allowance being made for some exceptional beauties and occasional originalities, there was not much in this 1827 volume to show the world that a new poetic power was about to arise ; its author's incomparable melody of rhythm

and haunting power of words were not, as yet, foreshadowed.

But this little book was suppressed, and its author,
in all probability, recalled to Richmond. Whatever
arrangements were made as to the future can only be
speculated upon—the result was, however, unless the
poet's most solemn word is to be doubted, that he
departed for Europe; and it is generally supposed, and
by Poe was never contradicted, in order to offer his
services to the Greeks against their Turkish tyrants.

## CHAPTER VII.

### EASTWARD HO!*

Towards the end of June, 1827, Edgar Poe would appear to have left the United States for Europe. It is very problematical whether he ever reached his presumed destination, the scene of the Greco-Turkish warfare, or ever saw aught, save in his " mind's eye," of

> " The glory that *was* Greece,
>     And the grandeur that *was* Rome."

The poems which he wrote either during his absence abroad or directly after his return home (such as " Al Aaraaf" and the " Sonnet to Zante "), contain allusions to Greece and its scenery that, in some instances, appear to be the result of personal reminiscence or impression; but with a mind of such identificative power as was Poe's, these coincidences cannot be allowed to count for much.

* This account of Poe's adventures in Europe is derived from *memoranda* made at his own request—during a dangerous illness which it was deemed might end fatally—shortly after his wife's decease. There does not appear to be any reason for doubting the accuracy of this any more than of any other of the poet's statements.—J. H. I.

Hannay says—and how many will agree with him ?—
" I like to think of Poe in the Mediterranean, with his
passionate love of the beautiful,—in ' the years of April
blood,'—in a climate which has the perpetual luxury
of a bath—he must have had all his perceptions of
the lovely intensified wonderfully. What he did there
we have now no means of discovering." * Poe had,
undoubtedly, been excited by the heroic efforts the
insurgent Greeks were making to throw off the yoke
of their Turkish oppressors, and was, probably, emulous
of Byron, whose example and Philhellenic poesy had
aroused the chivalric aspirations of the boys of both
continents, and whose writings, certainly, strongly influenced our hero's own muse at this epoch of his life.

Powell states that it was in conjunction with an
acquaintance, Ebenezer Berling, that the youthful poet
formed the design of participating in the Hellenic
revolution, and conjectures that Poe went alone in
consequence of his companion's heart failing him.†
Whatever may have been the truth with regard to
Berling, at that time the lad's most intimate and most
trusted acquaintance, it must be remembered that *he*
—unlike Poe the orphan—was a widow's only son,
and, doubtless, in delicate health, as he died not long
after his friend's departure.

* J. Hannay, *The Life and Genius of Edgar Allan Poe*, 1852.
† Powell, *Living Poets of America*, 1850.

A most interesting and suggestive memento of the youthful crusader's enthusiasm is to be found in an unknown translation by him of the famous " Hymn in honour of Harmodius and Aristogeiton." As an excuse for the omission of the latter hero's name, Poe pleads the impossibility of making it scan in English verse. If this juvenile version of these oft-translated verses does not display any very great poetic merit, it is at least as good, and, indeed, much better than many other renderings of the " Hymn " by well-known bards :—

" Wreathed in myrtle, my sword I'll conceal,
    Like those champions, devoted and brave,
When they plunged in the tyrant their steel,
    And to Athens deliverance gave.

" Beloved heroes ! your deathless souls roam
    In the joy breathing isles of the blest ;
Where the mighty of old have their home—
    Where Achilles and Diomed rest.

" In fresh myrtle my blade I'll entwine,
    Like Harmodius, the gallant and good,
When he made at the tutelar shrine
    A libation of Tyranny's blood.

" Ye deliverers of Athens from shame—
    Ye avengers of Liberty's wrongs !
Endless ages shall cherish your fame,
    Embalmed in their echoing songs."

Edgar Poe was absent from America on his Hellenic journey about eighteen months. The real adventures of his expedition have never, it is believed, been published. That he reached England is probable, although in the account of his travels, derived from his own dictation, that country was not alluded to any more than was the story of his having reached St. Petersburg, and there having been involved in difficulties that necessitated ministerial aid to extricate him. The latter incident is now stated to have occurred to his brother, William Henry Leonard, * whilst Edgar himself, it has been suggested by a writer claiming personal knowledge of him, resided for some time in London, formed the acquaintance of Leigh Hunt and Theodore Hook, and, like them, lived by literary labour.

According to Poe's own story—which apparently accounts only for a portion of his time—he arrived, eventually, at a certain seaport in France. Here he was drawn into a quarrel about a lady, and in a fight which ensued was wounded by his antagonist, a much more skilful swordsman than he was. Taken to his lodgings, and, possibly, ill tended, he fell into a fever. A poor woman, who attended to his needs and pitied him, made his case known to a Scotch lady of position, who was visiting the town in the hope of

* *Vide* Appendix B.

persuading a prodigal brother to relinquish his evil
ways and return home with her. This lady came to
see the wounded stranger, and for thirteen weeks had
him cared for, providing for all his wants, including
the attendance of a skilled nurse, whose place, indeed,
she often took herself. Whilst Poe was in a pre-
carious condition she visited him daily, and even
persuaded her brother to come and see the young
Englishman, as his language led them to believe he
was. When the patient became convalescent he was,
naturally, intensely grateful to his generous benefactor.
As the only means he possessed at that time of
showing his gratitude he wrote a poem to her, which
he entitled "Holy Eyes," with reference to the trust,
sympathy, and faith which he deemed her blue eyes
typical of. Indeed, according to Poe's description,
this lady's eyes were her chief personal attraction, she
being otherwise plain, large-featured, and old maidish.
Owing to the peculiarity of her position in this foreign
seaport, she did not wish her name made public, and
impressed this upon the youthful poet. She made
him promise to return to America—and perhaps supplied the means for him to do so—and adopt a profession, in which she expressed a hope of some day
hearing that he had become famous.

During his stay in France, so runs Poe's narration,
he wrote a novel, in which his own adventures were

described under the garb of fiction. The manuscript
of this story he carried back with him to America, and
retained it in his possession until, at least, some few
years before his death. When asked why he had not
published it, he replied that a French version of it
had been published, and had been accredited to Eugene
Sue, but that he would not sanction its publication in
English, because it was too sensational; that it was
not to his taste; that it had too much of the "yellow
cover novel style" for him to be proud of it, and,
moreover, that it contained "scenes and pictures so
personal, that it would have made him many enemies
among his kindred, who hated him for his vanity and
pride already, and in some respects very justly—the
faults of his early education." The truth in his story,
he asserted, was yet more terrible than the fiction.
"The Life of an Artist at Home and Abroad" was
the title by which Poe at one time designated this
youthful novel; it was written entirely in the third
person, and was pronounced by its author to be
"commonplace."

Such is the story dictated by Poe from what, it
was deemed at the time, might be his deathbed.
Whether it was fact, or fact and fiction deliriously interwoven, or mere fiction, invented in such a spirit of
mischief as, like Byron, he frequently indulged in at
the expense of his two inquisitive questioners, is, at

this late date, difficult to decide.  As he told the tale
to one whom he trusted, so it is here recounted.

After his long absence from home, if Mr. Allan's
residence may so be termed, Poe reached Richmond
safely in the beginning of March 1829, with little
besides a trunk load of books and manuscripts.  His
adopted mother had died during his absence: unfortunately he arrived too late to take a last farewell of
her, she having been interred the day before his arrival.
Mrs. Allan was buried in the family grave at Shockoe
Hill Cemetery, and a stone bearing the following in-
scription was erected over her remains:—

Sacred<br>
to the Memory of<br>
FRANCES KEELING ALLAN,<br>
who departed<br>
this transitory life<br>
on the Morning of the 28th of<br>
February 1829.<br>
This Monument is erected by<br>
JOHN ALLAN, her Husband,<br>
in testimony of his gratitude for her<br>
unabated affection to him,<br>
her zeal to discharge her domestic duties,<br>
and the fervour she manifested, both by<br>
precept and example,<br>
in persuading all to trust in the<br>
promises of the Gospel.

Apparently, the deceased lady had exercised a conciliatory influence in the Allan household, where, indeed, it is stated it was not unfrequently needed, and the poor tempest-tossed youth—who in after life always referred to her with affection—soon had to experience the effects of her loss. Mr. Allan does not appear to have manifested much pleasure at the prodigal's return, and it was not long before Poe again departed. He visited some of his paternal relatives, and is believed to have inspired one of his uncles, probably Mr. George Poe, with a belief in his genius. This relative seems to have taken some interest in his nephew's welfare, and at this time wrote to the late John Neal to solicit his confidential opinion as to the youth's poetic abilities. The reply was not altogether unfavourable, and the consequence of it was that Poe wrote to Neal, and proposed to publish a volume of poems dedicated to him. This proposition Neal sought to discourage, so far as regarded the intended dedication, contending that his unpopularity in the United States might injure the sale of the book. This remonstrance was not calculated to have much effect upon one of Poe's disposition—in fact, when shortly after this he published a new version of " Tamerlane," he dedicated it to his first literary correspondent.

After a short absence, the poet returned once more to Richmond, and it is within the recollection of Mr.

Bolling, his fellow-student at the University, that he accidentally met Poe the second night after he got back. The wanderer gave him a long account of the hardships he had had to endure, and what shifts he had been put to for a living, remarking that he had, as the only alternative for relief, betaken himself to authorship. The publication of "Al Aaraaf" was one result of this exertion. The poem, he informed his old friend, was then on sale at Sanxy's, a bookseller of Richmond, and he desired him to call there and obtain as many copies as he wished, adding, that should Bolling meet with any of their old college mates who would care to see the volume, he would like them presented with a copy, only it was to be presented as coming from Bolling, and not as from the author. The following day Poe accompanied his friend to Sanxy's store, gave him a copy of the book in question, and left the requisite instructions with the bookseller for Mr. Bolling to have as many more copies as he might require.

Previous to the publication of this, his first acknowledged collection of poems, Edgar Poe, as already remarked, wrote from Baltimore to John Neal, who was then editing *The Yankee*, in order to obtain his candid opinion of the forthcoming volume, sending him specimens of the contents. Through the columns of his paper, the editor replied, " If E. A. P. of Baltimore, whose lines about Heaven—though he professes to regard them as altogether superior to any in the whole range of American poetry, save two or three trifles referred to,—are, though nonsense, rather exquisite nonsense, would but do himself justice, he might make a beautiful, and perhaps a magnificent poem. There is a good deal to justify such a hope in—

> " ' Dim vales and shadowy floods—
> And cloudy-looking woods ;
> Whose forms we can't discover,
> For the trees that drip all over.
>
> The moonlight . . . . falls
> Over hamlets, over halls,
> Wherever they may be,
> O'er the strange woods, o'er the sea,
> O'er spirits on the wing,
> O'er every drowsy thing,
> And buries them up quite
> In a labyrinth of light.
> And then, how deep ! *Oh deep,*
> Is the passion of their sleep.'

We have no room for others."

In response to this praise—this faint first recognition of his ability *to do* something meritorious—Poe's gratitude and craving for sympathy prompted him to send the following letter :—

"I am young — not yet twenty — am a poet—if deep worship of all beauty can make me one—and wish to be so in the common meaning of the word. I would give the

world to embody one half the ideas afloat in my imagination.
(By the way, do you remember, or did you ever read, the
exclamation of Shelley about Shakespeare, 'What a number
of ideas must have been afloat before such an author could
arise!')    I appeal to you as a man that loves the same
beauty which I adore—the beauty of the natural blue sky
and the sunshiny earth—there can be no tie more strong
than that of brother for brother.  It is not so much that they
love one another, as that they both love the same parent—
their affections are always running in the same direction—
the same channel, and cannot help mingling.  I am, and have
been from my childhood, an idler.  It cannot therefore be
said that—

> " 'I left a calling for this idle trade,
>     A duty broke—a father disobeyed '—

for I have no father—nor mother.

"I am about to publish a volume of 'Poems'—the greater
part written before I was fifteen.  Speaking about 'Heaven'
the editor of *The Yankee* says, ' He might write a beautiful,
if not a magnificent poem ' — (the very first words of
encouragement I ever remember to have heard).  I am very
certain that as yet I have not written *either*—but that I
*can*, I will take my oath—if they will give me time.

"The poems to be published are 'Al Aaraaf,' 'Tamerlane,'
one about four, the other about three hundred lines, with
smaller pieces.  'Al Aaraaf' has some good poetry and much
extravagance, which I have not had time to throw away.

" ' Al Aaraaf' is a tale of another world—the star discovered
by Tycho Brahe, which appeared and disappeared so suddenly
—or rather it is not a tale at all.  I will insert an extract about
the palace of its presiding deity, in which you will see that I
have supposed many of the lost sculptures of our world to

have flown (in spirit) to the star 'Al Aaraaf'— a delicate
place more suited to their divinity :—

" ' Upreared upon such height arose a pile,' &c." *

After this the youthful poet quotes another passage
of eight lines, beginning " Silence is the voice of God,"
and ending with " And the red woods are withering
in the sky," and then two lengthy passages from
" Tamerlane," and the following fourteen lines from an
untitled poem :—

> " If my peace hath flown away
> In a night—or in a day—
> In a vision—or in none—
> Is it therefore the less gone ?
> I am standing 'mid the roar
> Of a weather-beaten shore,
> And I hold within my hand
> Some particles of sand—
> How few ! and how they creep
> Through my fingers to the deep !
> My early hopes ?   No—they
> Went gloriously away,
> Like lightning from the sky
> At once—and so will I."

In acknowledgment of this communication, John
Neal gave Poe generous notice, at the same time
letting him know that, in his opinion, if the remainder
of " Al Aaraaf" and  " Tamerlane " was as good as the

* Here follow 32 lines from the poem of " Al Aaraaf."—J. H. I.

extracts given, with all their faults, to say nothing of the more valuable portions, their author " deserved to stand high, very high, in the estimation of the shining brotherhood." Whether Poe would do so, however, he opined must depend not so much upon his present as upon his future worth, and he exhorted him to attempts yet loftier and more generous, alluding,—these, of course, being Neal's own words,—" to the stronger properties of the mind—to the magnanimous determination that enables a youth to endure the present, whatever the present may be, in the hope or rather in the belief—the fixed, unwavering belief—that in the future he will find his reward."

It is, of course, quite impossible to imagine what view the young poet took of Neal's friendly criticism, but one thing is certain, and that is, that the literary correspondence thus cordially commenced continued in a similar sympathetic strain until Poe's death. The second printed but first published volume of Poe, to which the above correspondence refers, bears the following title-page :—

AL AARAAF,

TAMERLANE,

AND

MINOR POEMS.

By Edgar A. Poe.

Baltimore : Hatch and Dunning.

1829.

This volume—published, apparently, at the close of
the year—is stated to have been for private circulation.
It contains only sixty-six pages, and many of these are
merely extra leaves and bastard titles. The real contents include " Al Aaraaf," substantially as now printed,
and prefixed to it, but unnamed, the sonnet now styled
"To Science." The present version of "Tamerlane"
—then dedicated to John Neal—follows, and there-
after succeed ten "Miscellaneous Poems." These
included the lines now known as "Romance," but
then called "Preface;" the song, "I saw thee on
thy bridal day;" "The Lake," from the suppressed
volume of 1827, and seven other pieces. Six of
these latter are, save some slight variations, as still
published, but in the following lines, "To M——,"
appear three stanzas subsequently omitted, as well as
a few trifling alterations. The whole poem, as it
stands in the 1829 edition, reads thus :—

> "Oh ! I care not that my earthly lot
> Hath little of earth in it—
> That years of love have been forgot
> In the fever of a minute.

> " I heed not that the desolate
> Are happier, sweet, than I—
> But that *you* meddle with *my* fate
> Who am a passer-by.

" It *is* not that my founts of bliss
  Are gushing—strange ! with tears—
Or that the thrill of a single kiss
  Hath palsied many years—

" 'Tis not that the flowers of twenty springs,
  Which have withered as they rose,
Lie dead on my heart-strings
  With the weight of an age of snows.

" Nor that the grass—oh ! may it thrive !
  On my grave is growing or grown—
But that, while I am dead, yet alive
  I cannot be, lady, alone."

These somewhat indefinite stanzas are typical of
the whole of the fugitive pieces in the little book, and
are, as usual, characteristic of his life and idiosyncrasies;
—morbid sensibility to kindness, haunting regrets for
an unprofited past, and a hopeless, utterly despairing
dread of the future. These " Miscellanous Poems,"
labelled—

" My nothingness—my wants—
  My sins—and my contritions "—

are hinted at, in " Romance," as "*forbidden things*" in
ordinary hours, and were, but too probably, occupations
interdicted by his godfather. But from some suppressed lines in another piece, inscribed to an unknown
person, it is clear that no amount of authority would

have constrained him from pursuing his own subjects.
He exclaims, after bewailing his early hopes, and alluding to an intention of *disappearing altogether :*—

> " So young ! ah no—not now—
>   Thou hast not seen my brow,
>   But they tell thee I am proud—
>   They lie—they lie aloud—
>   My bosom beats with shame
>   At the paltriness of name
>   With which they dare combine
>   A feeling such as mine—
>   Nor Stoic ? I am not :
>   In the tenor of my lot
>   I laugh to think how poor
>   That pleasure " to endure ! "
>   What ! shade of Zeno !—I !
>   Endure !—no—no—defy."

And that he did *defy* all parental, or assumed parental,
power to suppress his poetic aspirations, it is easy to
comprehend.   But in "Spirits of the Dead" a more
faithful representation of his self-styled "funereal
mind" is to be found—a very portrayal in one stanza,
wherein he alludes to the living being overshadowed
by the *will* of the dead.   It was, indeed, a never-end-
ing phantasy with him, that death was not absolute
separation from life—that the dead were not wholly
heedless of the deeds of the living.

But the two long poems constituted the chief value

of the 1829 edition. "Al Aråf," or "Al Aaraaf," as
the poet preferred styling it, is designed by the
Mohammedan imagination as an abode wherein a
gentle system of purgatory is instituted for the benefit
of those who, though too good for hell, are not fitted
for heaven—

"Apart from heaven's eternity—and yet how far from hell!"

Poe chose to locate this intermediate region in a
star discovered, or rather examined, by Tycho Brahe
(and which it is now conjectured must have been
a sun in course of conflagration), that appeared
suddenly in the heavens, and after having rapidly
attained a brilliancy surpassing that of Jupiter, gradually disappeared and has never since been seen.*
This poem of "Al Aaraaf" abounds in happy and
melodious passages, and has never yet received its
due meed of praise: some portions of the lyrical
intermedial chant are exquisitely and musically
onomatopœial in construction. The revised version
of "Tamerlane," too, given in this volume, is in every
respect à great advance upon the previous printed
draft: besides its enhanced poetic value, it is also far
superior as a work of art, improved punctuation and
indented lines affording evidence of· more skilled
handicraft than that employed upon the former copy.

* *Vide* Mr. R. Proctor's *Myths and Marvels of Astronomy.*

## CHAPTER VIII.

### WEST POINT.

IN 1802, the founders of the young Republic saw the
necessity of officering their troops with skilled soldiers,
and, with a foresight their children have not always
shown, instituted the West Point Military Academy—
a military school in many respects equal to the best
of Europe. Education and subsistence are gratuitous,
and a monthly allowance of twenty-eight dollars is
made to each of the cadets, so as to place them, as it
were, beyond the *necessity* of appealing to relatives for
anything. The course of study covers a period of four
years, during which the student is placed under a
discipline little less rigid than that of a soldier on
active duty. The number of cadets is limited, and
very great interest is required, as will be readily comprehended, in order to obtain a nomination.

It was, doubtless, the prospect or promise of receiving a nomination to this institution that induced Poe
to return to Mr. Allan's. General Scott, and other
influential friends, interested themselves on the youth's

behalf, and eventually obtained him an appointment. According to the rules of the Military Academy, nominations are not given to candidates after they have attained their twenty-first birthday, consequently Poe was only just in time to receive his appointment. The West Point records show that he was admitted into the institution as a cadet on the 1st of July 1830.

At the time Poe was admitted, the Military Academy was anything but a suitable place for the residence of a high-spirited and sensitive youth. The discipline was not only of the most severe description, but the place itself was utterly unfit for the habits of growing lads. An inquiry having been made into the rules and regulations of the institution, in conse-quence of an excitement caused by the death of some of the cadets, the Board sent in a report to the Secretary of War, about a year previous to the poet's admission, in which, after the examination of special cases, they said, "With regard to all the cadets, how-ever, it may be averred, that they are constantly tasked to the utmost in the way of mental exertion, while from the nature of the climate, for very nearly an entire moiety of the year, they are, for all the pur-poses of recreation, debarred from the use of their limbs," and, to obviate this latter objection, a building for exercise was recommended.

Poe is declared to have entered upon his new

mode of living with customary energy—for the idleness which he vaunted to Neal was more in theory
than in practice—but he speedily discovered how
totally unsuited for him was the strict discipline and
monotonous training of such a place as West Point.
The wayward and erratic course of existence to which
he had been so long accustomed, as well as the fact
that he had for so long a time been sole master of his
own actions, rendered the restraints of the Academy
most galling; nevertheless, that docility and amiability
which he generally manifested towards those with
whom he came in personal contact, caused him to
become a general favourite and a not altogether
unhopeful cadet. One of his fellow-cadets, speaking
of Poe's inability to follow the mathematical requirements of the place, says, " His mind was off from the
matter-of-fact routine of the drill, which, in such a
case as his, seemed practical joking, on some ethereal
visionary expedition." " His utter inefficiency and
state of abstractness at that place " were, doubtless,
the reasons that caused this authority to deem him
" marked for an early death." *

Complaints of the severity of the rules frequently
crop up in the press of the period: *Niles' Register*
for September 19th, 1829, after remarking that

* Duyckinck's *Cyclopedia of American Literature*, vol. ii., Article
" Poe, E. A."

" each cadet is to remain four years at the institution, and then serve one year in the military establishment of the United States," goes on to state, " But the service is so strict, and the punishment so uniformly inflicted, that many are suspended or expelled before the expiration of the four years—and it is generally rather a small minority of the whole number that is seen to pass through the whole tour of service; " finally, the report declares that out of a total of 204 cadets only 26 are without black marks attached to their names.   Whether Poe would have been one of the " small minority " had not events occurred to render, in his own opinion, his withdrawal requisite, is a debateable subject.   According to the most circumstantial account furnished of his residence at West Point,* the poet's career in the Military Academy was one scarcely calculated to cover him with institutional honours ; but Mr. Thomas W. Gibson, its author—a fellow-cadet, and a fellow-prisoner at a subsequent Court-Martial—is occasionally so inaccurate in his memory of the facts, that the whole of his narrative must be received *cum granô salis.*

" Number 28 South Barracks," says Mr. Gibson, " in the last months of the year of our Lord 1830, was pretty generally regarded as a hard room.   Cadets who aspired to high stand-

---

* *Harper's New Monthly Magazine*, November 1867, pp. 754-756.

ing on the Merit Roll were not much given to visiting it, at
least in day-time. To compensate in some measure for this
neglect, however, the inspecting - officer was uncommonly
punctual in his visits, and rarely failed to find some subject
for his daily report of demerit. The old barracks have passed
away, and are now only a dream of stone and mortar ; but
the records of the sins of omission and commission of Number
28 and its occupants remain, and are piled carefully away
among the dusty archives of the Academy.

"Edgar A. Poe was one of the occupants of the room.
' Old P——' [Henderson ?] and the writer of this sketch
completed the household. . . . Poe at that time, though only
about twenty years of age, had the appearance of being much
older. He had a worn, weary, discontented look, not easily
forgotten by those who were intimate with him. Poe was
easily fretted by any jest at his expense, and was not a little
annoyed by a story that some of the class got up, to the
effect that he had procured a cadet's appointment for his son,
and the boy having died, the father had substituted himself
in his place. Another report current in the corps was that
he was a grandson of Benedict Arnold.* Some good-natured
friend told him of it, and Poe did not contradict it, but
seemed rather pleased than otherwise at the mistake.

"Very early in his brief career at the Point he established
a high reputation for genius, and poems and squibs of local
interest were daily issued from Number 28, and went the
round of the classes. One of the first things of the kind that
he perpetrated was a diatribe in which all of the officers of
the Academy, from Colonel Thayer down, were duly if not

* Arnold was Governor of West Point at the time when his treachery
to the Americans was discovered through the apprehension of Major
André.—J. H. I.

favourably noticed.   I can recall but one stanza.   It ran
thus :—

> " John Locke was a very great name ;
> Joe Locke was a greater ; in short,
> The former was well known to Fame,
> The latter well known to Report."

" Joe Locke, it may be remarked by way of explanation,
was one of the instructors of tactics, and *ex officio* Inspector of
Barracks, and supervisor of the morals and deportment of
cadets generally.   In this capacity it was his duty to report
to head-quarters every violation of the regulations falling
under his observation : a duty in which he was in nowise
remiss, as the occupants of Number 28 could severally testify.

"The studies of the Academy Poe utterly ignored.   I doubt
if he ever studied a page of Lacroix, unless it was to glance
hastily over it in the lecture-room while others of his section
were reciting.  .  .  .

" The result of one of these foraging parties after supplies
created for a time no little excitement in the South Barracks.
People had been burned and hung in effigy from time immemorial, but it was reserved for Number 28 to witness the
eating of a Professor in effigy.   It was a dark, cold, drizzling
night, in the last days of November, when this event came
off.   The brandy bottle had been empty for two days, and
just at dusk Poe proposed that we should draw straws—the
one who drew the shortest to go down to Old Benny's and
replenish our stock.   The straws were drawn, and the lot fell
on me.

" Provided with four pounds of candles and Poe's last
blanket for traffic (silver and gold we had not, but such as
we had we gave unto Benny), I started just as the bugle
sounded to quarters.   It was a rough road to travel, but I

knew every foot of it by night or day, and reached my place of destination in safety, but drenched to the skin. Old Benny was not in the best of humours that evening. Candles and blankets and regulation shoes, and similar articles of traffic, had accumulated largely on his hands, and the market for them was dull in that neighbourhood. His chicken-suppers and bottles of brandy had disappeared very rapidly of late, and he had received little or no money in return.

"At last, however, I succeeded in exchanging the candles and blanket for a bottle of brandy and the hardest-featured, loudest-voiced old gander that it has ever been my lot to en-counter. To chop the bird's head off before venturing into barracks with him was a matter of pure necessity ; and thus, in fact, old Benny rendered him before delivery. I reached the suburbs of the barracks about nine o'clock. The bottle had not as much brandy in it as when I left Old Benny's; but I was very confident I had not spilled any. I had carried the gander first over one shoulder and then over the other, and the consequence was, that not only my shirt-front but my face and hands were as bloody as the entire contents of the old gander's veins and arteries could well make them.

"Poe was on the look-out, and met me some distance from the barracks, and my appearance at once inspired him with the idea of a grand hoax. Our plans were perfected in an instant. The gander was tied, neck and feet and wings together, and the bloody feathers bristling in every direction gave it a nondescript appearance that would have defied recog-nition as a gander by the most astute naturalist on the conti-nent. Poe took charge of the bottle and preceded me to the room. 'Old P——' was puzzling his brains over the binomial theorem, and a visitor from the North Barracks was in the room awaiting the result of my expedition.

" Poe had taken his seat, and pretended to be absorbed in the mysteries of 'Leçons Françaises.' Laying the gander down at the outside of the door, I walked or rather staggered into the room, pretending to be very drunk, and exhibiting in clothes and face a spectacle not often seen off the stage.

" 'My God! what has happened?' exclaimed Poe, with well-acted horror.

" 'Old K——! Old K——!' I repeated several times, and with gestures intended to be particularly savage.

" 'Well, what of him?' asked Poe.

" 'He won't stop me on the road any more!' and I produced a large knife that we had stained with the few drops of blood that remained in the old gander. 'I have killed him!'

" 'Nonsense!' said Poe. 'You are only trying one of your tricks on us.'

" 'I didn't suppose you would believe me,' I replied, 'so I cut off his head and brought it into barracks. Here it is!' And reaching out of the door I caught the gander by the legs, and giving it one fearful swing around my head, dashed it at the only candle in the room, and left them all in darkness, with what two of them believed to be the head of one of the Professors. The visitor leaped through the window and alighted in the slop-tub, and made fast time for his own room in the North Barracks—spreading, as he went, the report that I had killed Old K——, and that his head was then in Number 28. The story gained ready credence, and for a time the excitement in barracks ran high. When we lit the candle again 'Old P——' was sitting in one corner a blank picture of horror, and it was some time before we could restore him to reason.

"The gander was skinned—picking the feathers off was out

of the question—and after taps we cut him up in small pieces and cooked him in a tin wash-basin, over an anthracite fire, without seasoning of any kind. It was perhaps the hardest supper on record, but we went through with it without flinching. We had set out to eat old K—— in effigy, and we did it ; whether he ever learned of the honours we paid him that night I never learned."

Comment on this melodramatic and journalistically wrought-out story is needless, unless it be to remark, that it presents a picture of life in the Military Academy of those days which, even if highly coloured, is, doubtless, to some extent representative. Mr. Gibson notes that "the impression left by Poe in his short career at West Point was highly favourable to him. If he made no fast friends, he left no enemies behind him. But up to that time he had given," in the opinion of his fellow-cadet, "no indication of the genius which has since secured for him a world-wide fame. His acquaintance with English literature," says Mr. Gibson, "was extensive and accurate, and his verbal memory wonderful. He would repeat both prose and poetry by the hour, and seldom or never repeated the same passage twice to the same audience."

Until the close of 1830, Poe would appear to have maintained, if not a very high, at all events, a respectable position in the institution. In November of that year the Inspector issued a warning to the cadets of the approaching semi-annual examination, and pointed

out that " if dismissed, strong and satisfactory reasons
will be required to obtain a restoration," showing
thereby that dismissal from the Academy was considered no unusual occurrence, nor an unpardonable
offence.   The young poet would appear to have passed
through the old year without committing any crime
sufficiently heinous to bring down upon his head the
threatened terrors.   On the 31st of December a Court-
Martial was ordered to meet on the following 7th of
January, and was subsequently adjourned until the
28th instant.   Up to the 7th of January Poe would
appear to have maintained his position in the Academy,
but by that date events appear to have occurred to
render him determined to leave the service.   He
wished to resign, but without the consent of parent or
guardian his resignation could not be accepted, and
Mr. Allan, it is declared, withheld the required permission.*   The second marriage of Mr. Allan to the
young and " beautiful Miss Patterson," soon after the
death of his first wife, and the birth of a son and
heir, it is presumed, influenced the poet's godfather in
withholding his consent.   A young wife, and the prospect of a young family, were undoubtedly sufficient
inducements for a man of Mr. Allan's temperament to
make him endeavour to retain his godson in a place
where his claims upon the home purse need be little

* Didier, *Life of E. A. Poe,* p. 44.

or nothing, and whence he could at once proceed to a profession without calling upon his guardian for any pecuniary or other aid. As usual, Poe had his own views upon the subject, and, with his customary impetuosity, took the decision into his own hands. His plan of proceeding and its result—evidently foreseen and desired by him—will be best comprehended by a recapitulation of the "orders" issued in his case pursuant to the General Court-Martial. It should, however, be pointed out, that had the prisoner pleaded "guilty" to all the charges made against him, some leniency might have been shown, and his dismission not have been ordered; but, in order to render his offence unpardonable, he entered a plea of "not guilty" to an easily proveable charge, and then, to render his case utterly hopeless, declined to plead.

"MILITARY ACADEMY ORDER No. 7.  "ENGINEER DEPARTMENT, WASHINGTON, *February* 8, 1831.

"At the General Court-Martial, of which Lieutenant Thomas J. Leslie, of the Corps of Engineers, is President, convened at West Point, New York, on the 5th ult., in virtue of Military Academy Order No. 46, dated the 31st December 1830, was arraigned and tried . . . . .

Cadet E. A. Poe.

"The Court next proceeded to the trial of Cadet E. A. Poe of the U. S. Military Academy on the following charges and specifications :—

"CHARGE 1st.—Gross neglect of duty.

"Specification 1st.—In this, that he, the said Cadet Poe, did absent himself from the following parades and roll-calls between the 7th January and 27th January 1831, viz., absent from evening parade on the 8th, 9th, 15th, 20th, 24th, and 25th January 1831 ; absent from *reveillé* call on the 8th, 16th, 17th, 19th, 21st, 25th, and 26th January 1831 ; absent from class parade on the 17th, 18th, 19th, 20th, 24th, and 25th January 1831 ; absent from guard mounting on the 16th January 1831, and absent from church parade on the 23rd January 1831 ; all of which at West Point, New York.

"Specification 2nd.—In this, that he, the said Cadet E. A. Poe, did absent himself from all his Academical duties between the 15th and 27th January 1831. . . .

"CHARGE 2nd.—Disobedience of orders.

"Specification 1st. — In this, that he, the said Cadet Poe, after having been directed by the officer of the day to attend church on the 23rd January 1831, did fail to obey such order ; this at West Point, New York.

"Specification 2nd. — In this, that he, the said Cadet Poe, did fail to attend the Academy on the 25th January 1831, after having been directed so to do by the officer of the day ; this at West Point, New York.

"To which charges and specifications the prisoner pleaded as follows :—To the 1st specification of the 1st charge 'Not Guilty;' to the 2nd specification of the 1st charge, 'Guilty;' and 'Guilty' to the 2nd charge and its specifications. . . .

"The Court, after mature deliberation on the testimony adduced, find the prisoner 'Guilty' of the 1st specification, 1st charge, and confirm his plea to the remainder of the charges and specifications, and adjudge that he, Cadet E. A. Poe, be *dismissed* the service of the United States. . . .

"The proceedings of the General Court-Martial . . . in the cases of Cadets ——, ——, E. A. Poe, ——, ——, have been laid before the Secretary of War and are approved. . .

"Cadet Edgar A. Poe will be *dismissed* the service of the United States, and cease to be considered a member of the Military Academy after the 6th March 1831."

During the trial ample evidence was adduced for the prosecution, and only one witness, Cadet Henderson, who "roomed" with the prisoner, and whose evidence amounted to nothing, appeared for the defence; Poe himself, indeed, declined to plead, and evidently had, deliberately, determined to leave the service. Upon the 7th of January the Court-Martial met to try various offenders; and upon the very next day, and every day up to the date of the adjourned sitting, he purposely absented himself from all duties! The fact most certainly was that, apart from his dislike to the military profession, he saw that his prospects of a wealthy inheritance were shattered, and he determined at once to seek a livelihood in a profession more in accordance with his natural tastes.

## CHAPTER IX.

*LITERATURE.*

FOR some time after leaving West Point, Poe appears to have lived in New York. A few months after he left the Military Academy, it was announced that a volume of his poems would be published by subscription at the price of two and a half dollars per copy. " Permission was granted," says Mr. Gibson, " by Colonel Thayer to the corps to subscribe for the book, and as no cadet was ever known to neglect any opportunity of spending his pay, the subscription was pretty nearly universal. The book was received with a general expression of disgust ; . . . . it contained not one of the squibs and satires upon which his reputation at the Academy had been built up. Few of the poems contained in that collection now appear in any of the editions of his works, and such as have been preserved have been very much altered for the better. For months afterwards quotations from Poe formed the standing material for jests in the corps, and his reputation for genius went down at once to zero." As Mr.

Gibson seems to have had to leave West Point at the same time as Poe, his reminiscences of the effects produced by the little volume are, doubtless, derived from hearsay; but, unlike his inaccurate account of the book itself, they are confirmed by other evidence. General George W. Cullum states,[*] "As Poe was of the succeeding class to mine at West Point, I remember him very well as a cadet. . . . While at the Academy he published a small volume of poems. . . . These verses were the source of great merriment with us boys, who considered the author cracked, and the verses ridiculous doggerel."

This 1831 collection does not contain any poem not included in the existing editions, but includes many variations from, and lines extra to, the pieces as now published ; the title-page reads thus :—

POEMS.

BY

EDGAR A. POE.

*" Tout le monde a raison."*—ROCHEFOUCAULD.

Second Edition.

New York: Elam Bliss.

1831.

The little book contained 124 pages, and was dedicated to the United States Corps of Cadets. Prefixed

[*] *Harper's New Monthly Magazine*, vol. xlv. p. 561.

to the poems was a lengthy letter to a " Mr. B——,"
apparently a mythical personage, dated " West Point,
1831."   The poet begins—

   " DEAR B——,—Believing only a portion of my former
volume to be worthy a second edition—that small portion I
thought it as well to include in the present book as to re-
publish by itself.   Nor have I hesitated to insert from the
' Minor Poems,' now omitted, whole lines, and even passages,
to the end that being placed in a fairer light, and the trash
shaken from them in which they were embedded, they may
have some chance of being seen by posterity.
   " It has been said, that a good critique on a poem may be
written by one who is no poet himself.   This, according to
*your* idea and *mine* of poetry, I feel to be false—the less
poetical the critic, the less just the critique, and the converse.
On that account, and because there are but few B——s in
the world, I would be as much ashamed of the world's
good opinion as proud of your own.   Another than
yourself might here observe, ' Shakespeare is in possession
of the world's good opinion, and yet Shakespeare is the
greatest of poets.   It appears then that the world judge
correctly ; why should you be ashamed of their favourable judgment ?'   The difficulty lies in the interpretation
of the word ' judgment ' or ' opinion.'   The opinion is the
world's, truly, but it may be called theirs as a man would
call a book his ; they did not originate the opinion, but it is
theirs.   A fool, for example, thinks Shakespeare a great poet
—yet the fool has never read Shakespeare.   But the fool's
neighbour, who is a step higher on the Andes of the mind,
whose head [that is to say, his more exalted thought] is too
far above the fool to be seen or understood, but whose feet

[by which I mean his every day actions] are sufficiently near to be discerned, and by means of which that superiority is ascertained, which *but* for them would never have been discovered—this neighbour asserts that Shakespeare is a great poet—the fool believes him, and that is henceforward his *opinion.* This neighbour's own opinion has, in like manner, been adopted from one above *him,* and so, ascendingly, to a few gifted individuals, who kneel around the summit, beholding face to face the master spirit who stands upon the pinnacle. . . .

"You are aware of the great barrier in the path of an American writer. He is read, if at all, in preference to the combined and established wit of the world. I say established; for it is with literature as with law or empire—an established name is an estate in tenure, or a throne in possession. Besides, one might suppose that books, like their authors, improve by travel—their having crossed the sea is, with us, so great a distinction. Our antiquaries abandon time for distance; our very fops glance from the binding to the bottom of the title-page, where the mystic characters which spell London, Paris, or Genoa, are precisely so many letters of recommendation.

"I mentioned just now a vulgar error as regards criticism. I think the notion that no poet can form a correct estimate of his own writings is another. I remarked before that in proportion to the poetical talent would be the justice of a critique upon poetry. Therefore a bad poet would, I grant, make a false critique, and his self-love would infallibly bias his little judgment in his favour; but a poet, who is indeed a poet, could not, I think, fail of making a just critique; whatever should be deducted on the score of self-love might be replaced on account of his intimate acquaintance with the subject; in short, we have more instances of false criticism than of just where one's own writings are the test, simply because we have more bad poets than good. There are, of course, many objections to what I say: Milton is a great example of the contrary; but his opinion with respect to the 'Paradise Regained' is by no means fairly ascertained. By what trivial circumstances men are often led to assert what they do not really believe! Perhaps an inadvertent word has descended to posterity. But, in fact, the 'Paradise Regained' is little, if at all, inferior to the 'Paradise Lost,' and is only supposed so to be because men do not like epics, whatever they may say to the contrary; and reading those of Milton in their natural order, are too much wearied with the first to derive any pleasure from the second.

"I dare say Milton preferred Comus to either—if so—justly.

"As I am speaking of poetry, it will not be amiss to touch slightly upon the most singular heresy in its modern history—the heresy of what is called, very foolishly, the Lake School. Some years ago I might have been induced, by an occasion like the present, to attempt a formal refutation of their doctrine; at present it would be a work of supererogation. The wise must bow to the wisdom of such men as Coleridge and Southey, but being wise, have laughed at poetical theories so prosaically exemplified.

"Aristotle, with singular assurance, has declared poetry the most philosophical of all writings *—but it required a Wordsworth to pronounce it the most metaphysical. He seems to think that the end of poetry is, or should be, instruction—yet it is a truism that the end of our existence is happiness; if so, the end of every separate part of our existence—everything connected with our existence—should

---

* Σπουδιοτάτων και φιλοσοφικοτατον γενος.

be still happiness. Therefore the end of instruction should be happiness; and happiness is another name for pleasure ;— therefore the end of instruction should be pleasure; yet we see the above-mentioned opinion implies precisely the reverse.

" To proceed : *cæteris paribus,* he who pleases is of more importance to his fellow-men than he who instructs, since utility is happiness, and pleasure is the end already obtained which instruction is merely the means of obtaining.

" I see no reason, then, why our metaphysical poets should plume themselves so much on the utility of their works, unless indeed they refer to instruction with eternity in view ; in which case, sincere respect for their piety would not allow me to express my contempt for their judgment ; contempt which it would be difficult to conceal, since their writings are professedly to be understood by the few, and it is the many who stand in need of salvation. In such case I should no doubt be tempted to think of the devil in Melmoth, who labours indefatigably, through three octavo volumes, to accomplish the destruction of one or two souls, while any common devil would have demolished one or two thousand.

" Against the subtleties which would make poetry a study —not a passion—it becomes the metaphysician to reason— but the poet to protest. Yet Wordsworth and Coleridge are men in years ; the one imbued in contemplation from his childhood, the other a giant in intellect and learning. The diffidence, then, with which I venture to dispute their authority would be overwhelming did I not feel, from the bottom of my heart, that learning has little to do with the imagination —intellect with the passions—or age with poetry.

> " ' Trifles, like straws, upon the surface flow,
>    He who would search for pearls must dive below,'

are lines which have done much mischief. As regards the

greater truths, men oftener err by seeking them at the
bottom than at the top ; the truth lies in the huge abysses
where wisdom is sought—not in the palpable palaces where
she is found. The ancients were not always right in hiding
the goddess in a well ; witness the light which Bacon has
thrown upon philosophy ; witness the principles of our divine
faith—that moral mechanism by which the simplicity of a
child may overbalance the wisdom of a man.

"We see an instance of Coleridge's liability to err, in his
'Biographia Literaria'—professedly his literary life and
opinions, but, in fact, a treatise *de omni scibili et quibusdam
aliis.* He goes wrong by reason of his very profundity, and
of his error we have a natural type in the contemplation of
a star. He who regards it directly and intensely sees, it is
true, the star, but it is the star without a ray—while he who
surveys it less inquisitively is conscious of all for which the
star is useful to us below—its brilliancy and its beauty.

"As to Wordsworth, I have no faith in him. That he
had in youth the feelings of a poet I believe—for there are
glimpses of extreme delicacy in his writings—(and delicacy is
the poet's own kingdom—his *El Dorado*)—but they have the
appearance of a better day recollected ; and glimpses, at best,
are little evidence of present poetic fire—we know that a few
straggling flowers spring up daily in the crevices of the glacier.

"He was to blame in wearing away his youth in contemplation with the end of poetising in his manhood. With
the increase of his judgment the light which should make
it apparent has faded away. His judgment consequently
is too correct. This may not be understood,—but the old
Goths of Germany would have understood it, who used to
debate matters of importance to their State twice, once
when drunk, and once when sober—sober that they might

not be deficient in formality—drunk lest they should be destitute of vigour.

" The long wordy discussions by which he tries to reason us into admiration of his poetry speak very little in his favour: they are full of such assertions as this (I have opened one of his volumes at random)—'Of genius the only proof is the act of doing well what is worthy to be done, and what was never done before'—indeed ? then it follows that in doing what is *un*worthy to be done, or what *has* been done before, no genius can be evinced ; yet the picking of pockets is an unworthy act, pockets have been picked time immemorial, and Barrington, the pickpocket, in point of genius, would have thought hard of a comparison with William Wordsworth, the poet.

" Again—in estimating the merit of certain poems, whether they be Ossian's or Macpherson's can surely be of little consequence, yet, in order to prove their worthlessness, Mr. W. has expended many pages in the controversy. *Tantæne animis ?* Can great minds descend to such absurdity ? But worse still : that he may bear down every argument in favour of these poems, he triumphantly drags forward a passage, in his abomination of which he expects the reader to sympathise. It is the beginning of the epic poem '*Temora.*' 'The blue waves of Erin roll in light. The mountains are covered with day. Trees shake their dusky heads in the breeze.' And this—this gorgeous, yet simple imagery, where all is alive and panting with immortality—this, William Wordsworth, the author of 'Peter Bell,' has *selected* for his contempt. We shall see what better he, in his own person, has to offer. Imprimis :

" ' And now she's at the pony's tail,
And now she's at the pony's head—

> On that side now, and now on this ;
> And, almost stifled with her bliss,
> A few sad tears does Betty shed. . . .
> She pats the pony, where or when
> She knows not, happy Betty Foy !
> Oh Johnny, never mind the Doctor !'

" Secondly :

> " ' The dew was falling fast, the—stars began to blink ;
> I heard a voice : it said, drink, pretty creature, drink !
> And, looking o'er the hedge, be—fore me I espied
> A snow-white mountain lamb, with a—maiden at its side.
> No other sheep were near—the lamb was all alone,
> And by a slender cord was—tether'd to a stone.'

" Now, we have no doubt this is all true : we *will* believe it, indeed, we will, Mr. W.   Is it sympathy for the sheep you wish to excite ?   I love a sheep from the bottom of my heart.

" But there are occasions, dear B——, there are occasions when even Wordsworth is reasonable.   Even Stamboul, it is said, shall have an end, and the most unlucky blunders must come to a conclusion.   Here is an extract from his preface—

" ' Those who have been accustomed to the phraseology of modern writers, if they persist in reading this book to a conclusion (*impossible !*) will, no doubt, have to struggle with feelings of awkwardness ; (ha ! ha ! ha !) they will look round for poetry (ha ! ha! ha ! ha !), and will be induced to inquire by what species of courtesy these attempts have been permitted to assume that title.'   Ha ! ha ! ha ! ha ! ha !

" Yet, let not Mr. W. despair ; he has given immortality to a waggon, and the bee Sophocles has transmitted to eternity a sore toe, and dignified a tragedy with a chorus of turkeys.*

---

* This is a mistake, as turkeys were unknown in Europe before the discovery of America, whence they were imported.—J. H. I.

"Of Coleridge, I cannot speak but with reverence. His towering intellect ! his gigantic power ! To use an author quoted by himself, '*J'ai trouvé souvent que la plupart des sectes ont raison dans une bonne partie de ce qu'elles avancent, mais non pas en ce qu'elles nient.*' And to employ his own language, he has imprisoned his own conceptions by the barrier he has erected against those of others. It is lamentable to think that such a mind should be buried in metaphysics, and, like the Nyctanthes, waste its perfume upon the night alone. In reading that man's poetry, I tremble like one who stands upon a volcano, conscious, from the very darkness bursting from the crater, of the fire and the light that are weltering below.

"What is poetry ?—Poetry ! that Proteus-like idea, with as many appellations as the nine-titled Corcyra ! 'Give me,' I demanded of a scholar some time ago, 'give me a definition of poetry.' '*Très - volontiers ;*' and he proceeded to his library, brought me a Dr. Johnson, and overwhelmed me with a definition. Shade of the immortal Shakespeare ! I imagine to myself the scowl of your spiritual eye upon the profanity of that scurrilous Ursa Major. Think of poetry, dear B——, think of poetry, and then think of Dr. Samuel Johnson ! Think of all that is airy and fairy-like, and then of all that is hideous and unwieldy ; think of his huge bulk, the Elephant ! and then—and then think of the Tempest—the Midsummer Night's Dream—Prospero—Oberon—and Titania !

"A poem, in my opinion, is opposed to a work of science by having, for its *immediate* object, pleasure, not truth ; to romance, by having, for its object, an *indefinite* instead of a *definite* pleasure, being a poem only so far as this object is attained ; romance presenting perceptible images with definite, poetry with *in*definite sensations, to which end music is an *essential*, since the comprehension of sweet sound is our most

indefinite conception. Music, when combined with a pleasurable idea, is poetry; music, without the idea, is simply
music; the idea, without the music, is prose, from its very
definitiveness.

" What was meant by the invective against him who had
no music in his soul ?

" To sum up this long rigmarole, I have, dear B——, what
you, no doubt, perceive, for the metaphysical poets as poets,
the most sovereign contempt. That they have followers
proves nothing—

> " ' No Indian prince has to his palace
> More followers than a thief to the gallows.' "

Apart from the fact that the theory herein enunciated as to the object and aim of poetry is one which
its author never through life deviated from, this letter
is valuable and most interesting as the earliest known
specimen of Poe's prose work. In the 1831 volume
it is followed by a poetical " Introduction " of sixty-
six lines, an expansion of the twenty-one lines of the
1829 " Preface." These additional verses were subsequently suppressed, but a portion of them is well
worthy preservation here, not only as a fair sample of
their youthful inditer's poetic powers, but also for
their autobiographical allusions :—

> " Succeeding years, too wild for song,
> Then rolled like tropic storms along,
> Where, though the garish lights that fly
> Dying along the troubled sky,

Lay bare, through vistas thunder-riven,
The blackness of the general heaven;
That very blackness yet doth fling
Light on the lightning's silver wing.

"For, being an idle boy lang syne,
Who read Anacreon and drank wine,
I early found Anacreon-rhymes
Were almost passionate sometimes—
And by strange alchemy of brain
His pleasures always turned to pain—
His naïveté to wild desire—
His wit to love—his wine to fire;
And so, being young and dipt in folly,
I fell in love with melancholy,
And used to throw my earthly rest
And quiet all away in jest.
I could not love except where Death
Was mingling his with Beauty's breath—
Or Hymen, Time, and Destiny
Were stalking between her and me. . . .

"But *now* my soul hath too much room—
Gone are the glory and the gloom;
The black hath mellowed into gray,
And all the fires are fading away.

"My draught of passion hath been deep—
I revelled, and I now would sleep—
And after drunkenness of soul
Succeeds the glories of the bowl—
An idle longing night and day
To dream my very life away. . . "

To those acquainted with Poe's history thus far,
the pathos of the four final lines of the second stanza
will not be overlooked. These idiosyncratic verses
are followed by the exquisite lyric "To Helen," * a poem
written in commemoration of Mrs. Stannard, as Poe
himself afterwards acknowledged; then comes the
earliest known version of "Israfel;" which is succeeded by "The Doomed City"—a poem afterwards
improved and re-christened "The City in the Sea"—
expanded and weakened versions of "Fairyland," and
"The Sleeper," follow; next comes "A Pæan," chiefly
remarkable as being the germ of that melodious, exul-
tant defiance of death—"Lenore"—and then, finally,
so far as the "Miscellaneous Poems" are concerned,
some lines entitled "The Valley Nis"—ultimately
revised and published as "The Valley of Unrest."

The collection concludes with expanded reprints of
"Al Aaraaf," and "Tamerlane," but the additions and
variations are, generally, inferior in poetic value to the
earlier versions. Ultimately, upon their next republication, the poet's more matured judgment caused
him to curtail the proportions of most of the pieces
in this "second edition," by discarding the so strangely
added new lines. It should also be noted, in connection with this 1831 volume, that the punctuation is
not so good nor so characteristic as in its immediate

* Beginning, "Helen, thy beauty is to me."

predecessor, and that the whole book has the appearance of having been very hastily prepared for the press.

The profits, if any, on his "Poems," could not have sufficed long for Poe's maintenance, and, indeed, in a very short space of time he appears to have retraced his journey to Richmond. Upon his arrival at Mr. Allan's he did not receive a very gracious reception, as may be readily imagined, from his godfather's second wife. Mr. Allan, he was told, was confined to his bed by severe illness, and his request to be admitted to the sick man's chamber was refused. Excited by the refusal, he quarrelled with Mrs. Allan and left the house—the only home he had ever known—for ever, and in wrath. Mr. Allan was informed of the visit, and his godson's conduct was, apparently, represented to him in anything but favourable colours, for he wrote an angry letter forbidding him the house. The poet answered in a similar spirit, and never again, it is believed, held any further communication with his adopted father—with the man whom he had been taught to look to for aid and support, and whose property he had been led to believe was destined to be his own inheritance. All was over now, and he who a short time before had been regarded as the spoilt child of Fortune, was now homeless and penniless!

All attempts hitherto made to explain what Poe did, and whither he wandered, during the next two years succeeding his expulsion from his godfather's home, have signally failed. The assertion that he was residing at Baltimore with his aunt, Mrs. Clemm, is not in accordance with fact, her correspondence proving *that she never did know* where her nephew was during this interregnum in his history, and the poet himself does not appear to have ever afforded any reliable clue to the truth. Powell, in his well-meaning, but somewhat imaginative, sketch of Poe, asserts that the chivalrous youth left Richmond with the intention of offering his services to the Poles in their heroic struggle against Russia. Another biographer, of proven unreliability, suggests that Poe enlisted in the army, but after a short service deserted, although, in a previous sketch of the poet, this same writer stated that during the period referred to the youth endeavoured to subsist by authorcraft, only " his contributions to the journals attracted little attention, and his hopes of gaining a livelihood by the profession of literature were nearly ended at length in sickness, poverty, and despair." Other attempts, all more or less romantic, have been made to bridge over this chasm in Poe's life, but none possess such probability as that last cited. In no portion of his career did the poet prove the waters of Helicon Pactolian, and in his earliest efforts to obtain a subsistence by literary labour it almost necessarily follows—considering the then position of American letters—that his exertions were fruitless.

Poe's place of abode has not been discovered from the time he left Richmond in 1831 until the autumn of 1833, when he is again heard of as in Baltimore, and in apparently very straightened circumstances. It has been stated * that Poe was at this time residing with Mrs. Clemm in Cove Street, but, according to the Baltimore Directories—which are far better evidence than any personal memory—that lady resided in Wilks Street in 1831-2, and thence removed to No. 3 Amity Street, whilst extant correspondence proves that her nephew did *not* reside with her then, and, apparently, that he never lived with her until *after* his marriage. During this mysterious interval in the poet's life, it is claimed that he wrote the earlier versions of some of his finest stories, and even had some of them accepted and published, but not paid for, by contemporary editors. He himself stated in a note to the " MS. Found in a Bottle," that that tale was originally published in 1831, but the last figure is probably a misprint for 3.

In the autumn of 1833, the proprietors of the *Saturday Visiter*, a weekly literary journal, started in Baltimore the previous year, and then under the editorial charge of Mr. L. A. Wilmer, offered prizes of

* E. L. Didier, *Life of E. A. Poe*, p. 50.

one hundred dollars and fifty dollars respectively, for the best story and the best poem.  This offer coming to the knowledge of Poe, he selected six of his tales, and some lines—which he christened "The Coliseum" —out of a drama he was writing, and sent them to the committee appointed to inspect the manuscripts.  After a careful consideration of the various contributions received, the adjudicators, three well-known gentlemen, unanimously decided that those by Edgar Poe—a stranger to them all—were entitled to both premiums, but subsequently were induced, it is stated, to award the lesser prize to another competitor, in consideration of Poe having gained the larger amount.

Not content with this award, the adjudicators even went out of their way to draw up and publish the following flattering critique on the merits of the writings submitted by Poe, and published it in the *Saturday Visiter*, on the 12th of October 1833 :—

"Amongst the prose articles were many of various and distinguished merit, but the singular force and beauty of those sent by the author of 'The Tales of the Folio Club' leave us no room for hesitation in that department.  We have accordingly awarded the premium to a tale entitled the 'MS. Found in a Bottle.'  It would hardly be doing justice to the writer of this collection to say that the tale we have chosen is the best of the six offered by him.  We cannot refrain from saying that the author owes it to his own reputation, as well as to the gratification of the community, to publish the entire volume ('Tales of the Folio Club'). These tales are eminently distinguished by a wild, vigorous, and poetical imagination, a rich style, a fertile invention, and varied and curious learning.

(Signed)   JOHN P. KENNEDY.
J. H. B. LATROBE.
JAMES H. MILLER."

From Mr. Latrobe's reminiscences of the award and its result, written to a correspondent soon after the poet's decease, it is learned that he, Mr. Latrobe, was the reader of the manuscripts adjudicated upon, and that the little volume of tales submitted by Poe proved to be so enthralling, and so very far superior to anything else before the committee, that they read it through from beginning to end, and had no hesitation whatever in awarding the first prize to the author. "Our only difficulty," says Mr. Latrobe, "was in selecting from the rich contents of the volume."

Mr. Kennedy, the author of "Horse-Shoe Robinson," and other popular works, was so interested in the successful but unknown competitor, that he invited him to his house. Poe's response, written in his usual beautiful, clear caligraphy, proves into what a depth of misery he had sunk. How his heart bled to pen these words, few probably can imagine :—

"Your invitation to dinner has wounded me to the quick. I cannot come for reasons of the most

humiliating nature—my personal appearance. You
may imagine my mortification in making this dis-
closure to you, but it is necessary."

Impelled by the noblest feelings Mr. Kennedy at
once sought out the unfortunate youth, and found him,
as he records in his diary, friendless and almost starving.   Poe's wretched condition inspired the kind-
hearted author with pity, as did his palpable genius
with admiration, and henceforward he became a sincere and disinterested friend.   So far from contenting
himself with mere courtesies, Mr. Kennedy assisted his
new *protégé* to re-establish himself in the world, and
in many respects treated him more like an esteemed
relative than a chance acquaintance.   In his diary he
records, "I gave him . . . . . . free access to my table, and
the use of a horse for exercise whenever he chose; in
fact, brought him up from the very verge of despair."
Aided by such a friend, Poe's affairs could not but
begin to improve.

On the 27th March 1834 Mr. Allan died, in the
54th year of his age, and was interred beside his first
wife in Shockoe Hill Cemetery.   If Poe retained any
lingering hope of inheriting any portion of his godfather's wealth, he was at last undeceived, as his name
was not even mentioned in the will.   Aided, however,
by his new-made literary friends, and the reputation of
his recent success, the young poet now began to earn

his own livelihood. Mr. Kennedy relates that he set him "drudging upon whatever may make money," but Poe, as the moth to the candle, could not altogether refrain from the still "forbidden things" of poesy, and "when an hour with .calmer wings" intervened, returned to work upon his long commenced tragedy of "Politian."

The incidents of this drama were suggested by real events connected with Beauchampe's murder of Sharp, the Solicitor-General of Kentucky, the facts of which celebrated case are fully as romantic as the poet's fiction. Poe appears to have written a portion of "Politian" as early at least as 1831, and to have first published some fragments of it in the *Southern Literary Messenger* of 1835–36 as "Scenes from an Unpublished Drama." From the poet's manuscript copy* is seen the fact that this tragedy had been nearly, if not quite, completed, and although youthful *niaiseries* in some parts of this—the first draft, apparently—might have been justifiably excised, it cannot but be a subject for deep regret that the entire drama was not eventually published. As a rule, it must be conceded that the scenes selected and published by Poe were decidedly the most poetical, yet there are several very interesting and even meritorious passages in the manuscript that need not have been discarded. The omission of the humorous characters was no great loss,

* Now my property.—J. H. I.

but the transformation of Politian from "a young and noble Roman," and "his friend," Baldazzar, into English noblemen, was in no way necessary to, and certainly did not increase the *vraisemblance* of, the play.

That "Politian" has attracted less attention than its author's other poetical works is not strange; unequal in execution, a fragment, and a mystery, the public naturally passed it by. Monsieur Hughes, it is true, when he translated it into French, spoke of it as a tragedy "*où vivent des caractères vraiment humains,*" but he appears to have been the only person who has had a good word to say for it. This same author, moreover, draws attention to the noteworthy fact that the hero of the drama is, to some extent, and in some of his idiosyncrasies, a reflex of the author himself; "*comme tous les grands ecrivains,*" he remarks, "*Edgar Poe prête aux personnages qu'il met en scène ses sensations et ses sentiments personnel.*" In the third (of the published) scenes occur the following words of Politian's, which M. Hughes draws attention to as words that might well stand for Poe's own response to advising friends :—

> "What would'st thou have me do?
> At thy behest I will shake off that nature
> Which from my forefathers I did inherit;
> Which with my mother's milk I did imbibe,
> And be no more Politian, but some other."

"Give not thy soul to dreams," is the counsel of Baldazzar, and he bids him seek befitting occupa-. tion in the court or camp. "Speak no more to me," responds Politian, "of thy camps and courts. I am sick, sick, sick, even unto death !" he exclaims, "of the hollow and high-sounding vanities of the populous earth !" And further, when intimating that he is about to engage in a hostile encounter, Poe himself is seen clearly through his hero's words when he cries—

> "I *cannot* die, having within my heart
> So keen a relish for the beautiful."

And in a later scene are words so intensely Poësque that it needs no stretch of fancy to deem the poet speaking on his own behalf :—

> "Speak not to me of glory !
> I hate—I loathe the name ; I do abhor
> The unsatisfactory and ideal thing. . . .
> Do I not love—art thou not beautiful—
> What need we more ?  Ha ! glory ! now speak not of it :
> By all I hold most sacred and most solemn—
> By all my wishes now—my fears hereafter—
> By all I scorn on earth and hope in heaven—
> There is no deed I would more glory in,
> Than in thy cause to scoff at this same glory
> And trample it under foot."

One of the most interesting facts connected with

this early draft—almost as fine a specimen of Poe's exquisite caligraphy as is his latest manuscript—is that it contains, in the form of a soliloquy uttered by Politian, the lines published as "The Coliseum."

In August of 1834, the *Southern Literary Messenger,* a publication soon to be connected with Poe's fortunes, was started at Richmond, Virginia, by Mr. Thomas W. White, an energetic and worthy man. Such a magazine was a very hazardous speculation for that time ; it was started in opposition to the advice of its promoter's friends, and, but for a fortunate accident, might have caused his ruin.

After the magazine had passed through an erratic existence of some few months, its proprietor appealed to various well-known writers for literary aid, and amongst others, Mr. Kennedy was solicited; but he, being otherwise engaged, recommended Poe to send something. Acting upon this suggestion, our poet sent his manuscript "Tales of the Folio Club," and Mr. White's editor, Mr. James E. Heath, it is believed, greatly pleased with their style, alluded to them in very flattering terms in the *Messenger.*

In March 1835, "Berenice," Poe's first contribution, appeared in the new periodical, and the editor called marked attention to it and its author in these words : "Whilst we confess that we think there is too much German horror in his subject, there can be but

one opinion as to the force and elegance of his style."
This editorial idea of "Berenice" was not far from
the truth, as regards the mere literary value of the
work; but although its horrible *dénouement* is too
disgusting for even the genius of Poe to render palat-
able, for those who have obtained an insight into its
author's mental history it is one of the most remarkable, as it is also one of the earliest, of his tales.
No writer of repute has more thoroughly unbosomed
the secrets of his imagination, and more clearly disclosed the workings of his brain, than has Edgar Poe,
and in none of his writings have these autobiographic
glimpses been more abundantly vouchsafed than in
this story of "Berenice;" indeed, it may be better
described as an essay on its author's idiosyncrasies
than as a tale.

Among the various peculiarities of the early draft of
this work—some of which disappeared in the later
versions—it will be noted by his readers, is the first
development of Poe's assumed belief in metempsychosis,
a doctrine that, in subsequent writings, he recurred to
again and again, and which, it is scarcely assuming
too much to say, at times he evidently partially
believed in. One of the suppressed passages alludes
to its hero's "immoderate use of opium," a drug which
Poe occasionally resorted to, at least in after years,
even if he had not then already essayed its powers.

It is noteworthy to find him declaring, in 1845, in connection with De Quincey's "Confessions of an English Opium-Eater," "there is yet room for a book on opium-eating, which shall be the most profoundly interesting volume ever penned." Returning to an analysis of "Berenice"—that "Berenice" who is depicted as the hero's *cousin*—we find, as in so many of his youthful works, constant allusions to hereditary traits and visions of ancestral glories; but these boyish dreams are not, as generally supposed, referable to paternal but to maternal bygone splendours: to Arnheim—to the *hold* or *home* of the Arns (*i.e.*, the Arnolds)—to the Arnheim of the first and of the last of his stories. But perhaps the most representative —the almost prophetic—record of its author's idiosyncrasies, the trait which through after life would have most faithfully portrayed him, is contained in these words of the tale : "In the strange anomaly of my existence, feelings with me had never *been* of the heart, and my passions *always* were of the mind."

In the next month, April, appeared "Morella," one of Poe's favourite stories, and one which elicited from the Editor of the *Messenger* the comment that, whilst it would unquestionably prove its author's "great powers of imagination, and a command of language seldom surpassed," yet called forth the "lament that he has drunk so deep at some enchanted fountain, which seems to blend in his fancy the shadows of the tomb with the clouds and sunshine of life." "Morella," amid much that is typical, alludes to that all over-powering and overshadowing horror of Poe's life, to the notion that the consciousness of our identity is not lost at death, and that sentience survives the entombment. The early version of this tale contained "a Catholic hymn," which subsequently, much revised, appeared as a separate poem.

Mr. Kennedy had now had eighteen months' experience of Poe without discovering anything to alter the favourable opinion he originally formed of him, and he thus expressed himself to Mr. White on the subject :—

"BALTIMORE, *April* 13, 1835.

"DEAR SIR,—Poe did right in referring to me. He is very clever with his pen—classical and scholar-like. He wants experience and direction, but I have no doubt he can be made very useful to you. And, poor fellow! he is *very* poor. I told him to write something for every number of your magazine, and that you might find it to your advantage to give him some permanent employ. He has a volume of very bizarre tales in the hands of ——, in Philadelphia, who for a year past has been promising to publish them. This young fellow is highly imaginative, and a little given to the terrific. He is at work upon a tragedy, but I have turned him to drudging upon whatever may make money, and I have no doubt you and he will find your account in each other."

In the May number of the *Messenger* appeared
"Lionizing," one of the "Folio Club Tales," and on
the 30th of the same month its author is stated to
have said in a letter to Mr. White:—

"In regard to my critique of Mr. Kennedy's novel I
seriously feel ashamed of what I have written. I fully intended to give the work a thorough review and examine it
in detail. Ill health alone prevented me from so doing. At
the time I made the hasty sketch I sent you, I was so ill as
to be hardly able to see the paper on which I wrote, and I
finished it in a state of complete exhaustion. I have not,
therefore, done anything like justice to the book, and I am
vexed about the matter; for Mr. Kennedy has proved himself
a kind friend to me in every respect, and I am sincerely
grateful to him for many acts of generosity and attention.
You ask me if I am perfectly satisfied with your course. I
reply that I am entirely. My poor services are not worth
what you give me for them."

Besides his intercourse with Mr. Kennedy, Poe, says
Mr. Latrobe (who will be recollected as another of the
*Saturday Visiter's* Committee), "at my instance called
upon me sometimes, and entered at length into the
discussion of subjects on which he proposed to employ
his pen. When he warmed up he was most eloquent.
. . . He seemed to forget the world around him, as wild
fancy, logical truth, mathematical analysis, and wonderful combination of facts, flowed in strange comming-
ling from his lips, in words choice and appropriate, as

though the result of the closest study. I remember being particularly struck with the power that he seemed to possess of identifying himself with whatever he was describing. He related to me all the facts of a voyage to the moon, I think (which he proposed to put upon paper), with an accuracy of minute detail, and a truthfulness as regarded philosophical phenomena, that impressed you with the idea that he had just returned from the journey."

The voyage to the moon referred to by Mr. Latrobe is the famous " Hans Pfaall," or " Phaall," as it was originally spelt, which appeared in the June number of the *Messenger*, and created quite a *furor* at the time. Three weeks after the appearance of Poe's story, the notorious "Moon Hoax" of Richard Adams Locke was published by the *New York Sun ;* and both *jeux d'esprit* were presumed, by some journalists, to have been the work of one author. As even now some confusion exists between the respective dates of publication of the ephemeral hoax and the immortal story, Poe's own version, corroborated by independent evidence, shall be given:—

" About six months before this occurrence,[*] the Harpers had issued an American edition of Sir John Herschel's 'Treatise on Astronomy,' and I had been much interested

---

[*] *I.e.,* The publication of Mr. Locke's *Moon Hoax.*

in what is there said respecting the possibility of future lunar investigations. The theme excited my fancy, and I longed to give free rein to it in depicting my day-dreams about the scenery of the moon—in short, I longed to write a story embodying these dreams. The obvious difficulty, of course, was that of accounting for the narrator's acquaintance with the satellite; and the equally obvious mode of surmounting the difficulty was the supposition of an extraordinary telescope. I saw at once that the chief interest of such a narrative must depend upon the reader's yielding his credence in some measure as to details of actual fact. At this stage of my deliberations, I spoke of the design to one or two friends—to Mr. John P. Kennedy, the author of 'Swallow Barn,' among others—and the result of my conversations with them was, that the optical difficulties of constructing such a telescope as I conceived were so rigid and so commonly understood, that it would be in vain to attempt giving due verisimilitude to any fiction having the telescope as a basis. Reluctantly, therefore, and only half convinced (believing the public, in fact, more readily gullible than did my friends), I gave up the idea of imparting very close verisimilitude to what I should write—that is to say, so close as really to deceive. I fell back upon a style half plausible, half bantering, and resolved to give what interest I could to an actual passage from the earth to the moon, describing the lunar scenery as if surveyed and personally examined by the narrator. In this view I wrote a story which I called 'Hans Pfaall,' publishing it about six months afterwards in *The Southern Literary Messenger.*

"It was three weeks after the issue of the *Messenger* containing 'Hans Pfaall,' that the first of the 'Moon Hoax' editorials made its appearance in the *Sun*, and no sooner had I seen the paper than I understood the jest, which not for a moment could I doubt had been suggested by my own *jeu d'esprit.* Some of the New York journals (the *Transcript* among others) saw the matter in the same light, and published the 'Moon Story' side by side with 'Hans Pfaall,' thinking that the author of the one had been detected in the author of the other. Although the details are, with some exception, very dissimilar, still I maintain that the general features of the two compositions are nearly identical. Both are *hoaxes* (although one is in a *tone* of mere banter, the other of downright earnest) ; both hoaxes are on one subject, astronomy ; both on the same point of that subject, the moon ; both professed to have derived exclusive information from a foreign country ; and both attempt to give plausibility by minuteness of scientific detail. Add to all this, that nothing of a similar nature had ever been attempted before these two hoaxes, the one of which followed immediately upon the heels of the other.

"Having stated the case, however, in this form, I am bound to do Mr. Locke the justice to say, that he denies having seen my article prior to the publication of his own ; I am bound to add, also, that I believe him.

"Immediately on the completion of the 'Moon Story' (it was three or four days in getting finished), I wrote an examination of its claims to credit, showing distinctly its fictitious character, but was astonished at finding that I could obtain few listeners, so really eager were all to be deceived, so magical were the charms of a style that served as the vehicle of an exceedingly clumsy invention.

"It may afford even now some amusement to see pointed out those particulars of the hoax which should have sufficed to establish its real character. Indeed, however rich the imagination displayed in this fiction, it wanted much of the force which might have been given it by a more scrupulous attention to general analogy and to fact. That the public were misled, even for an instant, merely proves the gross ignorance which is so generally prevalent upon subjects of an astronomical nature."

The singular blunders to which he referred included a literal reproduction, in a winged man-bat, of Peter Wilkins' flying islanders, and it is impossible to refrain from expressing, with Poe, our wonder at the prodigious *success* of the hoax.

"Not one person in ten discredited it," he says, "and, (strangest point of all!) the doubters were chiefly those who doubted without being able to say why — the ignorant, those uninformed in astronomy — people who *would not* believe because the thing was so novel, so entirely 'out of the usual way.' A grave professor of mathematics in a Virginian college told me seriously that he had *no doubt* of the truth of the whole affair! The great effect wrought upon the public mind is referable, first, to *the novelty of the idea;* secondly, to the fancy-exciting and reason-repressing character of the alleged discoveries; thirdly, to the consummate tact with which the deception was brought forth; fourthly, to the exquisite *vraisemblance* of the narration. The hoax was circulated to an immense extent, was translated into various languages—was even made the subject of (quizzical) discussion in astronomical societies; drew down upon itself the grave denunciations of Dick,* and was, upon the whole, decidedly the greatest *hit* in the way of *sensation*—of merely popular

---

* Dr. Thomas Dick, the well-known astronomical writer.—J. H. I.

sensation—ever made by any similar fiction either in America or in Europe.

"Having read the 'Moon Story' to an end," continues Poe, "and found it anticipative of all the main points of my 'Hans Pfaall,' I suffered the latter to remain unfinished. The chief design in carrying my hero to the moon was to afford him an opportunity of describing the lunar scenery, but I found that he could add very little to the minute and authentic account *of Sir John Herschel.* The first part of 'Hans Pfaall,' occupying about eighteen pages of the *Messenger*, embraced merely a journal of the passage between the two orbs, and a few words of general observation on the most obvious features of the satellite; the second part will most probably never appear. I did not think it advisable even to bring my voyager back to his parent earth. He remains where I left him, and is still, I believe, 'the man in the moon.'"

Had Poe carried out his design of describing lunar scenery, what a rich feast of fantasy would have been provided for his admirers! A slight glimmering of the gloomy glories he intended to portray is afforded by some passages in what he did complete. "Fancy," says he,\* "revelled in the wild and dreamy regions of the moon. Imagination, feeling herself for once unshackled, roamed at will among the ever-changing wonders of a shadowy and unstable land. Now there were hoary and time-honoured forests, and craggy precipices, and waterfalls tumbling with a loud noise into abysses without bottom. Then I came suddenly

---

\* *Tales of the Grotesque and Arabesque*, vol. ii. pp. 68, 69. 1840 edit.

into still noonday solitudes where no wind of heaven ever intruded, and where vast meadows of poppies, and slender, lily-looking flowers, spread themselves out a weary distance, all silent and motionless for ever. Then again I journeyed far down, away into another country, where it was all one dim and vague lake, with a boundary line of clouds. And out of this melancholy water arose a forest of tall eastern trees like a wilderness of dreams. And I bore in mind that the shadows of the trees which fell upon the lake remained not on the surface where they fell—but sunk slowly and steadily down, and commingled with the waves, while from the trunks of the trees other shadows were continually coming out, and taking the place of their brothers thus entombed. 'This then,' I said thoughtfully, 'is the very reason why the waters of this lake grow blacker with age, and more melancholy as the hours run on.' But fancies such as these were not the sole possessors of my brain. Horrors of a nature most stern and most appalling would frequently obtrude themselves upon my mind, and shake the innermost depths of my soul with the bare supposition of their possibility. Yet I would not suffer my thoughts for any length of time to dwell upon these latter speculations."

After the publication of " Hans Pfaall," Mr. White seems to have determined to obtain, if possible, the exclusive services of his talented contributor. Editor after editor had assisted in managing the *Messenger* for a few months, and had then relinquished the onerous but not very remunerative task: Messrs. Heath, Tucker, Sparhawk, and others had followed in rapid succession, until, in June, Mr. White, again editorless, bethought him of Poe, and in answer to his inquiries, received these words :—" You ask me if I would be willing to come on to Richmond if you should have occasion for my services during the coming winter. I reply that nothing would give me greater pleasure. I have been desirous for some time past of paying a visit to Richmond, and would be glad of any reasonable excuse for so doing. Indeed, I am anxious to settle myself in that city, and if, by any chance, you hear of a situation likely to suit me, I would gladly accept it, were the salary even the merest trifle. I should, indeed, feel myself greatly indebted to you, if through your means I could accomplish this object. What you say in the conclusion of your letter, in relation to the supervision of proof-sheets, gives me reason to hope that possibly you might find something for me to do in your office. If so, I should be very glad—for at present only a very small portion of my time is employed."

Meanwhile, Mr. White having succeeded in obtaining the aid of another *littérateur*, who promised " to devote his exclusive attention " to the editorial work of the *Messenger*, was in no hurry to complete an

arrangement with Poe, who, however, contributed to the
July number "The Visionary"—a tale afterwards retitled
"The Assignation"—and these lines "To Mary":—

> " Mary, amid the cares—the woes
>        Crowding around my earthly path,
>    (Sad path, alas ! where grows
>    Not ev'n one lonely rose),
>        My soul at least a solace hath
>    In dreams of thee, and therein knows
>    An Eden of sweet repose.

> " And thus thy memory is to me
>        Like some enchanted, far-off isle,
>    In some tumultuous sea—
>    Some lake beset as lake can be
>        With storms—but where, meanwhile,
>    Serenest skies continually
>        Just o'er that one bright island smile."

To the August *Messenger* Poe contributed the sar-
castic sketch of "Bon-Bon," and "The Coliseum :
Prize Poem from the *Baltimore Visiter.*" By this
time the new editor, who had assisted at the gestation
of two numbers of Mr. White's magazine, followed the
example of his numerous predecessors and retired,
whereupon our poet was invited to Richmond to assist
in the editorial duties, at a salary of five hundred and
twenty dollars per annum.

At the very moment when Poe received this offer, he
was arranging with Mr. L. A. Wilmer for the publica-

tion, in co-operation with that gentleman, of a literary magazine or newspaper in Baltimore. Some correspondence had already passed between the two young *literati*, and Poe, says Mr. Wilmer, "proposed to join with me in the publication of a monthly magazine of a superior, intellectual character, and had written a prospectus, which he transmitted to me for examination." Mr. White's proposition completely demolished the project, for, as both the promoters of it were devoid of pecuniary means, Poe immediately accepted the proffered post, and thus, as his intended partner remarks, " the grand intellectual illumination we had proposed to make in Baltimore was necessarily postponed." *

Upon revisiting the abode of his earlier days, and in circumstances so altered from those of yore, the unfortunate poet was afflicted with a terrible melancholia—an affliction which frequently beset him on his journey through life, and which was, apparently, not merely the natural outcome of privation and grief, but also to some extent hereditary. Writing to his friend Kennedy to acquaint him with the fact of his appointment on the *Messenger*, he says :—

" RICHMOND, *September* 11, 1835.

" DEAR SIR,—I received a letter from Dr. Miller, in which he tells me you are in town. I hasten, therefore, to

---

* L. A. Wilmer, *Our Press Gang*, p. 35.

write you, and express by letter what I have always found it impossible to express orally—my deep sense of gratitude for your frequent and ineffectual assistance and kindness. Through your influence Mr. White has been induced to employ me in assisting him with the editorial duties of his magazine at a salary of five hundred and twenty dollars per annum. The situation is agreeable to me for many reasons, but, alas! it appears to me that nothing can give me pleasure, or the slightest gratification. Excuse me, my dear sir, if in this letter you find much incoherency. My feelings at this moment are pitiable, indeed. I am suffering under a depression of spirits such as I never felt before. I have struggled in vain against the influence of this melancholy; *you will believe me* when I say that I am still miserable in spite of the great improvement in my circumstances. I say you will believe me, and for this simple reason, that a man who is writing for *effect* does not write thus. My heart is open before you; if it be worth reading, read it. I am wretched, and know not why. Console me—for you can. But let it be quickly, or it will be too late. Write me immediately; convince me that it is worth one's while—that it is at all necessary to live, and you will prove yourself indeed my friend. Persuade me to do what is right. I do mean this. I do not mean that you should consider what I now write you a jest. Oh, pity me! for I feel that my words are incoherent; but I will recover myself. You will not fail to see that I am suffering under a depression of spirits which will ruin me should it be long continued. Write me then and quickly; urge me to do what is right. Your words will have more weight with me than the words of others, for you were my friend when no one else was. Fail not, as you value your peace of mind hereafter.     E. A. POE."

To this saddening wail of despair Kennedy responded :—

" I am sorry to see you in such plight as your letter shows you in. It is strange that just at this time, when everybody is praising you, and when fortune is beginning to smile upon your hitherto wretched circumstances, you should be invaded by these blue devils. It belongs, however, to your age and temper to be thus buffeted—but be assured, it only wants a little resolution to master the adversary for ever. You will doubtless do well henceforth in literature, and add to your *comforts*, as well as to your reputation, which it gives me great pleasure to assure you is everywhere rising in popular esteem."

Notwithstanding his "blue devils," as his friend phrased it, the new editor worked wonders with the *Messenger*. "His talents," records Kennedy, "made that periodical quite brilliant while he was connected with it," and indeed, within little more than a twelve-month from Poe's appointment in the following December, as sole editor, the circulation increased from seven hundred to nearly five thousand—an increase quite unparalleled at that time in the history of this class of magazines. The success was, of course, due to the originality and fascination of Poe's stories, and the fearlessness of his trenchant critiques.

The *Messenger* for September contained the " Loss of Breath," and "King Pest," two of Poe's poorest stories : the latter is one of those quizzical hoaxes upon

which he sometimes squandered his genius, and upon
which his readers have frequently wasted their time
in vain attempts to discover meanings not discoverable
because not existent.    The same number which completed the first volume also contained " Shadow," one
of its author's phenomenal prose poems, and these
" Lines written in an Album : "—

> " Eliza ! let thy generous heart
>    From its present pathway part not ;
> Being everything which now thou art,
>    Be nothing which thou art not.
>
> So with the world thy gentle ways—
>    Thy unassuming beauty—
> And truth—shall be a theme of praise
>    For ever—and love a duty."

The " Eliza," in whose album these lines were
written, was the daughter of Mr. White; after her
father's death in 1842 she was an occasional and esteemed visitor at the house of the poet, spending many
months with his wife and aunt at their Fordham home.

In the December number of the *Messenger*, at
Mr. White's instance apparently, he commenced that
system of literary scarification—that crucial dissection
of bookmaking mediocrities—which, whilst it created
throughout the length and breadth of the States terror
of his powerful pen, at the same time raised up

against him a host of implacable, although unknown, enemies, who henceforth never hesitated to accept and repeat any story, howsoever improbable, to his discredit. It would have been far better for his future welfare and fame if, instead of affording contemporary nonentities a chance of literary immortality by impaling them upon his pen's sharp point, he had devoted the whole of his time to the production of his wonderful tales and still more wondrous poems.

The second volume of the *Messenger* began in December, and, among other contributions by the new editor, contained a crushing critique on a work styled " Norman Leslie." This was the first of those reviews already alluded to that did their author so much injury —personal and posthumous. In the initial number of 1836 appeared various critical articles, and the singular tale of metempsychosis, " Metzengerstein." In the early version of this fiction the poet introduced some of those family reminiscences he was wont to intersect his writings with : after stating that the death of the hero's father was quickly followed by that of his mother, he exclaims, with as much prophetic as retrospective truth, " How *could* she die ?—and of consumption ! But it is a path I have prayed to follow. I would wish all I love to perish of that gentle disease. How glorious ! to depart in the heyday of the young blood—the heart all passion—the imagination all fire—amid the remembrances of happier days !"

The next issue of the *Messenger* contained various critiques—including an eulogistic one of Bulwer—the story of the "Duke de l'Omelette," and the first part of Poe's papers on "Autography," the second appearing in a subsequent number. The amusement, excitement, and ill-temper these articles aroused will be best gathered from the author's own subsequent account of the *jeu d'esprit :*—

"Some years ago there appeared, in the *Southern Literary Messenger*, an article which attracted very general attention, not less from the nature of its subject, than from the peculiar manner in which it was handled. The editor introduces his readers to a certain Mr. Joseph Miller, who, it is hinted, is not merely a descendant of the illustrious Joe of jest-book notoriety, but is that identical individual in proper person :—

"The object of his visit to the editor is to place in his hands the autographs of certain distinguished American *literati*. To these persons he had written rigmarole letters on various topics, and in all cases had been successful in eliciting a reply. The replies only (which it is scarcely necessary to say are all fictitious) are given in the Magazine with a genuine autograph facsimile appended, and are either burlesques of the supposed writer's usual style, or rendered otherwise absurd by reference to the nonsensical questions imagined to have been propounded by Mr Miller.

"With the public this article took amazingly well, and many of our principal papers were at the expense of reprinting it with the woodcut autographs. Even those whose names had been introduced, and whose style had been burlesqued, took the joke, generally speaking, in good part. Some of them were at a loss what to make of the matter. Dr. W. E. Channing of Boston was at some trouble, it is said, in calling to mind whether he had or had not actually written to some Mr. Joseph Miller the letter attributed to him in the article. This letter was nothing more than what follows :—

" 'Boston, ——.

" ' Dear Sir,—No such person as Philip Philpot has ever been in my employ as a coachman, or otherwise. The name is an odd one, and not likely to be forgotten. The man must have reference to some other Doctor Channing. It would be as well to question him closely.—Respectfully yours,
" ' W. E. Channing.

" ' To Joseph X. Miller, Esq.'

" The precise and brief sententiousness of the divine is here, it will be seen, very truly adopted or ' hit off.'

" In one instance only was the *jeu d'esprit* taken in serious dudgeon. Colonel Stone and the *Messenger* had not been upon the best of terms. Some one of the Colonel's little brochures had been severely treated by that journal, which declared that the work would have been far more properly published among the quack advertisements in a square corner of the *Commercial*. The Colonel had retaliated by whole-sale vituperation of the *Messenger*. This being the state of affairs, it was not to be wondered at that the following epistle was not quietly received on the part of him to whom it was attributed :—

"'NEW YORK, ——.

"'DEAR SIR,—I am exceedingly and excessively sorry that it is out of my power to comply with your rational and reasonable request. The subject you mention is one with which I am utterly unacquainted. Moreover, it is one about which I know very little—Respectfully,

"'W. L. STONE.

"'JOSEPH V. MILLER, Esq.'

"These tautologies and anti-climaces were too much for the Colonel, and we are ashamed to say that he committed himself by publishing in the *Commercial* an indignant denial of ever having indited such an epistle.

"The principal feature of this autograph article, although perhaps the least interesting, was that of the editorial comment upon the supposed MSS., regarding them as indicative of character. In these comments the design was never more than semi-serious. At times, too, the writer was evidently led into error or injustice through the desire of being pungent—not unfrequently sacrificing truth for the sake of a *bon mot*. In this manner qualities were often attributed to individuals, which were not so much indicated by their handwriting, as suggested by the spleen of the commentator. But that a strong analogy *does* generally and naturally exist between every man's chirography and character, will be denied by none but the unreflecting."

Poe's contributions to the remaining numbers of the *Messenger* for 1836 included, besides reprints of his poems, the "Pinakidia," or commonplace book notes, several critiques on contemporary books and authors, the story of "Epimanes"—now styled "Four Beasts

in One,"—a " Tale of Jerusalem," and a masterly
analysis of Maelzel's *soi-disant* " Automaton Chess-
player." In this last-named paper, the poet demonstrated by clear, concise, and irrefutable arguments,
that the machine then being exhibited before the
citizens of Richmond must be regulated in its operations by *mind*—that, in fact, it was no automaton at
all, but simply a piece of mechanism guided by human
agency.

# CHAPTER X.

## *MARRIAGE.*

EARLY in 1836, a gleam of hope broke in upon Poe's overclouded career. Amongst those of his father's kindred whom the poet had sought out at Baltimore was his aunt Maria, widow of Mr. William Clemm, a man who, it is stated, had expended his property on behalf of a not over-grateful country. Mrs. Clemm was in greatly reduced circumstances, but she proffered her brother's son such welcome as was in her power, and a strong mutual affection sprang up between the two relatives. Mrs. Clemm had an only child, her daughter Virginia, described by all parties as an exquisitely lovely and amiable girl. Virginia Clemm, born on the 13th of August 1822, was still a child when her handsome cousin Edgar revisited Baltimore after his escapade at West Point. A more than cousinly affection, which gradually grew in intensity, resulted from their frequent communion, and ultimately, whilst one, at least, of the two cousins was but a child, they were married.

In that beautiful allegory of his life — in his unrhymed rhapsody of "Eleonora" *—Poe tells in thrilling words how, ere the knowledge of his love had dawned upon him, he dwelt in a world of his own creative imagination, in the symbolic "Valley of the Many-Coloured Grass," apart from the outer and, to him, less real world. There they dwelt—he and his cousin and her mother—and there they, he and she, who was but a child, had dwelt for many years before consciousness of love had entered into their hearts, until one evening when their secret was unveiled to them, and so, murmurs the poet, "we spoke no words during the rest of that sweet day, and our words even upon the morrow were tremulous and few. . . . And now we felt enkindled within us the fiery souls of our forefathers. The passions which had for centuries distinguished our race came thronging with the fancies for which they had been equally noted, and together breathed a delirious bliss over the 'Valley of the Many-Coloured Grass.'" And then, in magic words, he tells of the revolution, wrought beneath the wizard spells of Love, of how "a change came o'er the spirit of *his* dream," and of how all things beautiful became more beauteous; how "strange, brilliant flowers burst out upon the trees where no flowers had been known before;" how the "tints of

* Published in *The Gift* in 1842.

the green grass deepened," and how a myriad things
of nature, before unnoted, bloomed and blossomed
into being.

Then is the delicate loveliness of his child-bride
compared by the poet to " that of the Seraphim," and
she was, he reminds himself, " a maiden artless and
innocent as the brief life she had led among the
flowers. No guile disguised the fervour of love which
animated her heart, and she examined with me its
inmost recesses as we walked together." Rarely, if
ever before, was poet blessed with so sweet a bride,
or with more artless affection than was Poe when he
acquired the heart and hand of her of whom he
sang—

> " And this maiden, she lived with no other thought
> Than to love and be loved by me."

It has been stated, but with palpable incorrectness,
that the young cousins were married in Baltimore on
the 2nd of September 1835, previous to Poe's departure for Richmond, but that the youthful pair did not
live together for more than a year, and that they were
again married in Richmond, where they were to reside, this second marriage ceremony taking place to
save comment, as the previous one had been so private.
This circumstantial romance must be consigned to the
limbo whence so many of the legends accumulated

round the poet's memory have been dismissed. The
facts are :—When it was learned that the young *littérateur* purposed marrying his cousin, who was still under
fourteen, her half-sister's husband—Edgar Poe's first
cousin—Mr. Neilson Poe, to hinder so premature a
marriage, offered her mother to receive Virginia into
his own family, and provide for her education, with
the understanding, that if after a few years the cousins
still entertained the same affection for each other,
they should be married. When Poe heard of this he
indited an earnest, passionate protest against the
arrangement to Mrs. Clemm, who, consequently, declined the offer, and the marriage soon afterwards took
place.

Edgar Poe was married to Virginia Clemm, in
Richmond, on the 6th of May 1836, and, says Mrs.
Clemm, Judge Stannard and his son Robert, Edgar's
old schoolfellow—were among the first callers. Mrs.
Clemm took up her residence with the young couple,
both so doubly related to her, and became as it were
their guardian and protector. But few weeks, however, had passed over the heads of the wedded pair
before darksome troubles began to hover over them :
" the fair and gentle Eulalie " had indeed become the
poet's " blushing bride," but it was a " dream too
bright to last " to deem the fatality which dogged his
footsteps had forsaken him. Some inkling of his

troubles may be gleaned from this letter to his friend Kennedy :—

"RICHMOND, VA., *June* 7, 1836.

" DEAR SIR,—Having got into a little temporary difficulty, I venture to ask you, once more, for aid, rather than apply to any of my new friends in Richmond.

" Mr. White, having purchased a new house, at $10,000, made propositions to my aunt to rent it to her, and to board himself and family with her. This plan was highly advantageous to us, and, having accepted it, all arrangements were made, and I obtained credit for some furniture, &c., to the amount of $200, above what little money I had. But upon examination of the premises purchased, it appears that the house will barely be large enough for one family, and the scheme is laid aside—leaving me now in debt (to a small amount) without those means of discharging it upon which I had depended.

" In this dilemma I would be greatly indebted to you for the loan of $100 for six months. This will enable me to meet a note for $100 due in three months—and allow me three months to return your money. I shall have no difficulty in doing this, as, beyond this $100, I owe nothing, and I am now receiving $15 per week, and am to receive $20 after November. All Mr. White's disposable money has been required to make his first payment.

" Have you heard anything further in relation to Mrs. Clemm's estate ?

"Our *Messenger* is thriving beyond all expectation, and I myself have every prospect of success.

" It is our design to issue, as soon as possible, a number of the Magazine consisting entirely of articles from our most distinguished *literati*. To this end we have received, and

have been promised, a variety of aid from the highest sources
—Mrs. Sigourney, Miss Sedgwick, Paulding, Flint, Halleck,
Cooper, Judge Hopkinson, Dew, Governor Cass, J. Q. Adams,
and many others. Could you not do me so great a favour as
to send a scrap, however small, from your portfolio? Your
name is of the greatest influence in that region where we
direct our greatest efforts—in the South. Any little reminiscence, tale, *jeu d'esprit*, historical anecdote—anything, in
short, *with your name*, will answer all our purposes.

"I presume you have heard of my marriage.—With
sincere respect and esteem, yours truly,

"EDGAR A. POE.

"J. P. KENNEDY."

The pecuniary embarrassment to which this communication alludes, even if temporarily relieved by his
friend, was doubtless of a chronic character, and
probably the chief cause of Poe quitting Richmond,
and resigning his connection with the *Literary Messenger*. Although he parted on friendly terms from
Mr. White, and in after years wrote and spoke of him
with kindliness, there is little doubt but that the
poet relinquished his post on the magazine in consequence of the rate of remuneration he received being
not only much less than he deemed his name and
*entire* services entitled him to, but even less than he
could decently maintain his household upon. The
number of the magazine for January 1837 was the
last *Messenger* under Poe's editorship, and it contained,

in addition to certain reviews and reprinted poems of
his, the first part of " Arthur Gordon Pym;" a second
instalment of the romance appearing in the following number, after its author's severance from the
periodical.

Previous to giving up charge of the *Messenger*, Poe,
with that thoughtfulness of friends which he often
manifested, wrote to Mr. Wilmer, to tell him of his
intention of leaving Richmond, and suggesting that
he, Wilmer, should come thither without delay, as he
was certain he could obtain the post he was about to
vacate.   Mr. Wilmer, however, could not avail himself of the offer, as he was preparing to leave for
Philadelphia.*

Apparently, Mr. White parted with his clever editor
with much reluctance, yet he could not, or he would
not, comply with his requirements — requirements,
indeed, it has been suggested, that included partnership in the publication.   In the number of the magazine containing Poe's resignation of the editorship,
announced in the words, " Mr. Poe's attention being
called in another direction, he will decline, with the
present number, the editorial duties of the *Messenger*,"
the proprietor issued a notice to the effect, that " Mr.
Poe, who has filled the editorial department for the
last twelve months with so much ability, retired from

* L. A. Wilmer, *Our Press Gang.*

that station on the 3rd instant," but will, so it was promised, "continue to furnish its columns from time to time with the effusions of his vigorous and popular pen."

How soon after this Poe left Richmond, and what he was doing for the next few months, are still unanswered questions. After the expiration of a short interregnum, he is discovered as settled in New York once more, and this time accompanied by his wife and her mother. During one portion, at least, of this residence in New York, the Poes lived at 113½ Carmine Street, where Mrs. Clemm attempted, as one method of lessening the household expenses, to keep a boarding house, but the experiment does not appear to have met with any success, and the family fell into very poor circumstances. An interesting account of the poet's limited *ménage* at this epoch of the story, has been given by the late William Gowans, the wealthy and eccentric bibliopolist, who boarded with Mrs. Clemm.*

Alluding to the untruthfulness of the prevalent idea of Poe's character, the shrewd old man remarks—

" The characters drawn of Poe by his various biographers and critics may with safety be pronounced an excess of exaggeration, but this is not to be much wondered at, when

---

* In the *New York Evening Mail*, December 1870.

it is taken into consideration that these men were rivals either as poets or prose writers, and it is well known that such are generally as jealous of each other as are the ladies who are handsome, or those who desire to be considered to be possessed of the coveted quality. It is an old truism, and as true as it is old, 'that in the midst of counsel there is safety.'

"I, therefore, will also show you my opinion of this gifted but unfortunate genius. It may be estimated as worth little, but it has this merit—it comes from an eye and ear witness; and this, it must be remembered, is the very highest of legal evidence. For eight months or more, 'one house contained us, us one table fed!' During that time I saw much of him, and had an opportunity of conversing with him often, and I must say, that I never saw him the least affected with liquor, nor even descend to any known vice, while he was one of the most courteous, gentlemanly, and intelligent companions I have met with during my journeyings and haltings through divers divisions of the globe; besides, he had an extra inducement to be a good man as well as a good husband, for he had a wife of matchless beauty and loveliness, her eyes could match that of any houri, and her face defy the genius of a Canova to imitate; a temper and disposition of surpassing sweetness; besides, she seemed as much devoted to him and his every interest as a young mother is to her first-born. . . . Poe had a remarkably pleasing and prepossessing countenance, what the ladies would call decidedly handsome."

Mr. Gowans—who is remembered as "one of the most truthful and uncompromising of men"—in conversing with Mr. Thomas C. Latto with reference to

Poe and his young wife, whom he described as fragile in constitution, but of remarkable beauty, testified that the poet " was uniformly quiet, reticent, gentlemanly in demeanour, and during the whole period he lived there, not the slightest trace of intoxication or dissipation was discernible in the illustrious inmate, who was at that time engaged in the composition of 'Arthur Gordon Pym.' Poe " kept good hours," he said, " and all his little wants were seen to by Mrs. Clemm and her daughter, who watched him as sedulously as if he had been a child." Mr. Gowans was a man of known intelligence, and, writes Mr. Latto, " being a Scotchman, is by no means averse to ' *a twa-handed crack*,' but he felt himself kept at a distance somewhat by Poe's aristocratic reserve." \* Mr. Gowans only left when the household was broken up, and the close connection which he was daily brought into with members of it, and the opportunity which he had of seeing what kind of life the poet was then leading, render his testimony valuable.

*Res augustœ domi* notwithstanding, the domestic life of the poet, at this period at least, was not altogether unhappy. As yet, the fact had not manifested itself to him that his girlish bride's beauty was but the signal of the fatal disease that she was destined to fall an early victim to; nor could he forbode,

---

\* In a letter to the late Mrs. Whitman, dated July 8th, 1870.

that she was to succumb to that fell complaint he
had erstwhile so rashly wished all he loved to perish
of.  A little while later and the devoted husband
learnt, as he bemoaned, that " the finger of death was
upon her bosom—that, like the ephemeron, she had
been made perfect in loveliness only to die."  Ever
since his marriage Poe had spent his leisure hours in
continuing his young wife's education, and under his
careful tuition she became highly accomplished.  " She
was an excellent linguist and a perfect musician, and
she was *so very beautiful,*" records her bereaved
mother.  "How often has Eddie* said, ' I see no one
so beautiful as my sweet little wife.' "

" Eddie," declares his " more than mother," " was
domestic in all his habits, seldom leaving home for an
hour unless his darling Virginia, or myself, were with
him.  He was truly an affectionate, kind husband,
and a devoted son to me.  He was impulsive, generous, affectionate, and *noble.*  His tastes were very
simple, and his admiration for all that was good and
beautiful very great. . . .  We three lived only for
each other." †

This epoch of quiet domestic happiness does not
appear to have been one very fruitful of literary produce, or, if it were, the result has been lost sight of.

* The poet's pet name at home.
† Letter to Judge Neilson Poe, August 19th, 1860.

During 1837 Poe contributed a critique of Stephens's "Incidents of Travel in Egypt, Arabia Petræa, and the Holy Land," to the October number of the *New York Review.* This Quarterly was a theological publication, and required a class of writing utterly unsuited to Poe's range of thought, he therefore wisely forbore from attempting anything of a similar kind again. His next literary essay was the completion of "The Narrative of Arthur Gordon Pym," the first and second instalments of which romance, as already pointed out, had appeared in the *Southern Literary Messenger.* The interest the work had aroused during its issue in the magazine determined Poe to complete it, that is to say, as far as he ever intended to complete it, the abrupt and unfinished state of its closing paragraph having, evidently, been intentional. The story was not issued in book form until July 1838. It is said that it did not excite much notice in America, but it was very successful in England, where, besides the authorised reprints of Messrs. Wiley and Putnam, several other editions were speedily disposed of. The truthful air of " The Narrative," and the circumstantiality of the title-page and preface, doubtless attracted attention, but indeed the whole romance is detailed with such Defoe-like minuteness—with such an apparent want of art—especially in lengthy, almost tedious, citations from presumable kindred works—that the reading public was bound to submit to the temporary fascination, and accept the *vraisemblance* for truth itself. The abrupt termination of "The Narrative," and the pretext alleged for it, both contributed greatly to the apparent fidelity to fact. The chief defect in the tale is the supernatural final paragraph—wisely omitted in the London reprint—which neither adds to the interest nor increases the life-like truthfulness. The original title-page of Poe's longest tale deserves reproduction here; it reads thus :—

"THE NARRATIVE
of
ARTHUR GORDON PYM,
of Nantucket ;
Comprising the Details of a Mutiny and Atrocious Butchery on Board the American Brig Grampus, on her way to the South Seas—with an Account of the Recapture of the Vessel by the Survivors; their Shipwreck, and subsequent Horrible Sufferings from Famine, their Deliverance by means of the British Schooner Jane Gray ; the brief Cruise of this latter Vessel in the Antarctic Ocean : her Capture, and the Massacre of her Crew among a Group of Islands in the 84th parallel of Southern Latitude, together with the incredible Adventures and Discoveries still further South, to which that distressing Calamity gave rise.

New York : Harper & Brothers.
1838."

Students of Poe's works who have learned to recognise his method of thought, know how frequently
he discloses his mental history in those parentheti-
cal passages he so much affected. In the above
narrative these disclosures, interwoven with autobiographical *data*, occur both oft and o'er. In the "preliminary notice," and in the first chapter of the
romance, fact and fiction are ingeniously blended, and
real and ideal personages are mingled somewhat con-
fusingly together. His readers are well aware how
clearly Poe's idiosyncrasies, both in his prose and in
his verse, show through the transparent masks behind
which his heroes are supposed to be hidden, and in
this "Narrative" it is rarely that the imaginary hero
is thought of otherwise than as identical with Poe
himself. The adventurous lad Pym is certainly not
the person to whom our thoughts tend when the
second chapter of this tale begins, "In no affairs of
mere prejudice, *pro* or *con*, do we deduce inferences
with entire certainty, even from the most simple *data*,"
and we are at no loss to comprehend the autobiographic fidelity of the author when he says, under the
pseudonym of Pym, "One of my enthusiastic temperament, and somewhat gloomy, although glowing imagination," and, "It is strange, too, that he most strongly
enlisted my feelings in behalf of the life of a seaman,
when he depicted his more terrible moments of suffer-

ing and despair. For the bright side of the painting
I had a limited sympathy."

Dreams of the day and of the night are plentiful
in Pym's narrative, and are rather more typical of the
psychological introspection of the poet than of the
healthy animalism and muscular energy of the sailor.
And yet they are not out of harmony with the tone
of this work, nor discordant with the overwrought
imagination of a sensitive youth. A dreaming fit is
described in the second chapter—that whence Pym is
aroused by the dog "Tiger"—which fully equals in
descriptive terror and power of language any of the
English Opium-Eater's "Confessions;" whilst the
analysis of the various mental phases through which
the hero passes—as told in Chapter xxiv.—from the
time he commences his descent of the soapstone cliff
and *must not think*, until the *longing to fall* is finally
finished by the fall, quite equals in psychological
subtlety anything that De Quincey ever did. Another
noteworthy passage is that in Chapter xxi, wherein
is described the horrible dread, ever recurring with
such ghastly effect in Poe's tales, of entombment alive :
"The supremeness of mental and bodily distress of
living inhumation" continually overshrouds his imagination, and his readers are goaded into believing that
the narrator himself must have experienced the so-
graphically-portrayed horrors of "the blackness of

darkness which envelops the victim, the terrific oppression of lungs, the stifling fumes from the damp earth," and all the appalling paraphernalia of a death-scene, which he shudderingly declares, even as he describes, are "not to be tolerated—never to be conceived."

The originality of Poe's genius, as shown in this "Narrative," will doubtless be the more generally admired, although less real, in such things as where he explains the singular character of the many-hued waters—which never seemed limpid—in the Antarctic island; and in the gradually-revealed horror of the inhabitants of the *colour white;* or in the ingenuity of the perusal of the torn letter by phosphorus; or in such probably inexplicable psychological facts, as the long ocean travelling voyager, in his delirium, beholding every creation of his "mind's-eye" in *motion*—movement being the all predominant idea. Our remarks on "Arthur Gordon Pym" are purposely directed more towards bringing prominently forward certain commonly unnoted characteristics of the tale, than to recalling attention to its generally appreciated, and frequently commented upon, more salient features.

Another of Poe's productions for this year was "Siope: A Fable. [In the manner of the Psychological Autobiographists]." "Siope," which appeared in the *Baltimore Book* for 1838, is the weird prose poem now styled " Silence," and is paralleled in many passages by its author's sonnet to " Silence " and other later poems.    Poe's inventive genius, indeed, was much more limited than is generally supposed, leading him to frequently repeat and repolish, rather than to originate, over and over again : the same favourite quotation, or pet idea, may be found doing duty in several places.    Those readers well acquainted with his earlier as well as later publications, will be able to recall to mind many instances of such repetition.

CHAPTER XI.

*IN THE CITY OF PENN.*

LATE in 1838 Poe removed to Philadelphia. The reason of his removal is uncertain, but it has been suggested that regular literary employment was proffered him in the Quaker city, wherefore, as the independence he had sought to earn by his pen was not obtainable in New York, he migrated thither with his *lares et penates.* That, or the constitutional restlessness, which like a fiend goaded him hither and thither, may have been the motive power. The whole burden of the household now falling upon his shoulders, for Mrs. Clemm relinquished the New York house and accompanied the Poes to Philadelphia, the poet sought engagements in various quarters. Among other magazines for which he agreed to write was the *American Museum,* a new publication projected and edited by Dr. N. C. Brooks of Baltimore. Requested by the proprietor to furnish a critique on Washington Irving, Poe replied in the following terms :—

"PHILADELPHIA, *September* 4, 1838.

"MY DEAR SIR,—I duly received your favour with the $10. Touching the review, I am forced to decline it just now. I should be most unwilling not to execute such a task well, and this I could not do at so short notice, at least now. I have two other engagements which it would be ruinous to defer. Besides this, I am just leaving Arch Street for a small house, and, of course, am somewhat in confusion.

"My main reason, however, for declining is what I first alleged, viz.: I could not do the review well at short notice. The truth is, I can hardly say that I am conversant with Irving's writings, having read nothing of his since I was a boy, save his 'Granada.' It would be necessary to give his entire works a reperusal. You see, therefore, the difficulty at once. It is a theme upon which I would like very much to write, for there is a vast deal to be said upon it. Irving is much overrated, and a nice distinction might be drawn between his just and his surreptitious and adventitious reputation—between what is due to the pioneer solely, and what to the writer.

"The merit, too, of his tame propriety and faultlessness of style should be candidly weighed. He should be compared with Addison, something being hinted about imitation, and Sir Roger de Coverley should be brought up in judgment. A bold and *a priori* investigation of Irving's claims would strike home, take my word for it. The American literary world never saw anything of the kind yet. Seeing, therefore, the opportunity of making a fine hit, I am unwilling to hazard your fame by a failure, and a failure would assuredly be the event were I to undertake the task at present.

"The difficulty with you is nothing—for I fancy you are conversant with Irving's works, old and new, and would not

have to read for the task. Had you spoken decidedly when I
first saw you, I would have adventured. If you can delay
the review until the second number I would be most happy
to do my best. But this, I presume, is impossible.

"I have gotten nearly out of my late embarrassments.
—— would not aid me, being much pushed himself. He
would, no doubt, have aided me, if possible. Present my
respects if you see him.—Very truly yours,
                              " EDGAR A. POE.

"Suppose you send me proofs of my articles ; it might be
as well—that is, if you have time. I look anxiously for the
first number, from which I date the dawn of a fine literary
day in Baltimore.

"After the 15th, I shall be more at leisure, and will be
happy to do you any literary service in my power. You have
but to hint.                              " E. A. P."

Whether Dr. Brooks made use of the suggestions
thrown out, and attempted something that would make
" a fine hit," matters little, but it is consolatory to
think that he had not " spoken decidedly when " the
poet first saw him, otherwise the world might have
had a not too charitable critique on the " surreptitious
and adventitious reputation" of Washington Irving,
in lieu of the weird story of " Ligeia," which was Poe's
contribution to the initial number of the periodical.

"Ligeia," the poet's favourite tale, was suggested,
he says,* *by a dream*—a dream in which the eyes

* In a MS. note, on a revised copy of the tale in my possession.—J. H. I.

of the heroine produced the intense effect described in the fourth paragraph of the work. "Ligeia," heralded by one of those splendid passages which begem Joseph Glanvill's "Essays," assumes for its motto, "Man doth not yield himself to the angels, nor unto death utterly, save only through the weakness of his feeble will." A theme more congenial to the dream-haunted brain of Poe could scarcely be devised; and in his exposition of the thoughts suggested by its application he has been more than usually successful. The failure of Death to annihilate Will was, indeed, a suggestion that the poet—dreadingly, despairingly, familiar as he was with charnel secrets—could not fail to grasp at with the energy of hope, and adorn with the funereal flowers of his grave-nourished fantasy. In Poe's gradual and unnoted steps towards proving the impossible possible, his reader's reason is fettered, and his mind is blinded to the impassible limits of nature with such careful art, that he loses all hold on fact, and is ready and willing for the nonce to credit the reality of any mental chimera the wizard chooses to conjure up. At the *dénouement* of such a tale, one feels as if awakening from a nightmare: the knowledge that it is fiction is still for a while overclouded with the horrible thought that *it might be true.*

Like most of Poe's other tales, "Ligeia" was frequently revised and altered, and did not originally contain, as it does now, that most weird and most original of all his poems, " The Conqueror Worm."

The two other literary engagements to which the poet alluded in his letter to Dr. Brooks were with the Pittsburgh *Literary Examiner* and the Philadelphia *Gentleman's Magazine.* The latter was the property of Mr. W. E. Burton, an Englishman, who obtained some reputation in his days as a comedian, and then attempted to add to it as a *littérateur,* an attempt in which he was scarcely so successful. Poe appears to have contributed some odds and ends to the *Gentleman's Magazine* almost from his first arrival in Philadelphia, but it was not until July of the following year, when he was appointed editor, that he published anything of note in its pages. In the last month of 1838, he contributed to the *Museum* "The Signora Zenobia," and its pendant "The Scythe of Time," afterwards respectively renamed " How to Write a Blackwood Article," and " A Predicament."

In *The Gift* for 1839 appeared " William Wilson," one of the poet's finest tales, and one in many parts confessedly autobiographical. In an eulogistic but discriminative review of Hawthorne, published in *Graham's Magazine,* Poe drew attention to certain incidents in " Howe's Masquerade " that might be deemed to resemble plagiarism from " William Wilson," and "*might be* a very flattering coincidence of thought " by his countryman ; but the strangest thing about it is, that Poe's own tale is most closely paralleled in plot by a rare drama, attributed to Calderon, called " El Encapo-tado," which Washington Irving had called attention to. The hero of the Spanish story, like " William Wilson," is throughout life thwarted in all his schemes for the acquisition of wealth, pleasure, or love, by a mysterious stranger, and when he ultimately forces the unknown, at the point of the sword, to unmask, his " Fetch " or *double* is beheld.* To accuse Poe of plagiarism in this case would be unjust, for the idea of the *dual man* permeates all civilised literatures, but it is a severe commentary upon some of his own ill-con-sidered critiques—which, however, have been most bitterly avenged.

The portions of " William Wilson " referring to the hero's school-days in England have already been trans-ferred to these pages, but there are other passages—evidently intended to be included in the writer's con-fessions—of interest here. Is it not Poe himself who says, " I long for the sympathy—I had nearly said for the pity—of my fellow-men. I would fain have them believe that I have been, in some measure, the slave of circumstances beyond human control. I would wish them to seek out for me some little oasis of *fatality* amid a wilderness of error. I would have

* *Vide* Medwin's *Life of Shelley*, vol. II, pp. 300, 301.

them allow—what they cannot refrain from allowing
—that although temptation may have erewhile
existed as great, man was never *thus*, at least, tempted
before?" The usual exaggerations of boyhood's reminiscences—those days all deem they remember so distinctly, yet as a rule describe so indefinitely—are well
marked in the portrayal of the old Stoke Newington
house and its accessories; but it is in the shadowy
suggestiveness of the two "William Wilsons'" similarity that the author's power is displayed. The
"singular whisper" of the one boy which grew to be "the
very echo" of his namesake's; the coincidence of birth-
days and of names; the non-observance of the resemblance by the other pupils; the gradually increasing
aversion for the wise monitions proffered by his *alter
ego*, and the terrible signification of the one "William
Wilson" *being asleep*, when his bedside was visited by
the other, on the last night of his stay in the Academy,
are all strokes of a master's hand—of a master who
stands alone and incomparable in the realm he has
himself constructed.

To the *Museum* for January and February Poe
contributed "Literary Small Talk," and to the April
number his much-admired lyric, "The Haunted Palace."
With respect to this latter arose a controversy similar
to that suggested by "Howe's Masquerade:" as with
that, so with this, Poe, it is alleged, deemed he had

been copied, and that Longfellow's " Beleaguered City "
was a plagiarism of his idea, and is stated to have
referred to the undeniable fact that his poem appeared
first, Longfellow's not being published until November 1839, when it appeared in the *Southern Literary
Messenger.*   Of all men *literati* should be the first to
recognise the fact that human invention is not infinite,
and that similar ideas frequently occur almost simul-
taneously to different persons, it is, therefore, both
rational and just to assume the resemblance between
the poems of Poe and Longfellow to have been accidental.   At all events, a similar fantasy to theirs had
been embodied in Tennyson's " Deserted House," published as early as 1830.

"The House of Usher," another of the poet's *chefs
d'œuvre,* illustrative of belief—a belief shared by
many of the good and great—in the sentience of all
matter, was published in the September number of
the *Gentleman's Magazine,* to which publication, as
already remarked, Poe had been appointed editor.
Mr. White, of the *Literary Messenger,* alluding in his
October issue to the tale and its author, remarks—
" We are pleased to find that our old assistant,
Edgar A. Poe, is connected with Burton in the editorial management of the *Gentleman's Magazine.*   Mr.
Poe is favourably known to the readers of the
*Messenger* as a gentleman of fine endowment; possess-

ing a taste classical and refined. . . We always pre-
dicted that Mr. Poe would reach a high grade in
American literature;" only, adds his former employer,
" we wish Mr. Poe would stick to the department of
criticism; *there*, he is an able professor." It was this
" sticking to criticism," to oblige publishers, instead
of following the true bent of his genius, that ruined
Poe's personal reputation, and lost the world many a
priceless poem and wondrous tale.

In the " Fall of the House of Usher," is developed
one of its author's favourite methods of riveting his
reader's attention. As in so many of his stories, instead
of soliciting sympathy for himself as the hero, he the
rather would appear to repel it, by assuming the
*rôle*, in his person of narrator, of a somewhat matter-
of-fact, even commonplace, practical character, in no
way *en rapport* with the eccentric or visionary friend
who is the real hero. He, Poe, pretends to come
before the stage, or to remain on it only in the minor
character of " Chorus," and thus casts a further air
of reality on the personages he introduces, by deluding
his readers into the belief that they are but fellow
spectators with him. Nevertheless, in the character
of " Roderick Usher"—a character upon which the
poet lavished his most consummate art, and upon
whose surroundings he bestowed the wealth of his
own desires—is sought to be depictured what Poe

wished the world to believe he resembled, as Byron did with his "Corsairs" and "Laras." The opium-eating hypochondriac, the *Fear*-fearing monomaniac, is less unlike the veritable author of "Ulalume" than is the friend of "Usher;" the mesmeriser of "Valdemar;" the associate of "Legrand" of "the Gold Bug;" the cool man of the world, who only represents the conventional half—*the side turned to the public.*

Poe's other contributions to the *Gentleman's Magazine,* during the remainder of 1839, were not of an important character, consisting chiefly of short book notices, slight sketches to accompany engravings, and reprints of his shorter poems. "William Wilson" and "Morella" were also republished in its pages, and in the December number appeared "The Conversation of Eiros and Charmion." This tale, in some respects resembling one entitled "The Comet," which had appeared in *The Token* for 1839, describes the history of this earth's destruction by a comet, and is supposed to be told in Aidenn by Eiros to Charmion. The final catastrophe is assumed to take place through the *total extraction of the nitrogen* from our atmosphere, and the consequent immediate and omnipresent combustion of the world. The whole story is most weirdly suggestive, and the climax startling in the extreme.

Under the title of *Tales of the Grotesque and Arabesque,* Poe now published a collection of his stories, in two volumes. These tales were copyrighted in 1839, but the title-page is dated 1840, and bears upon it the motto from Goethe :—

> "Seltsamen Tochter Jovis,
> Seinem Schosskinde, der Phantasie."

The volumes are inscribed to "Colonel William Drayton, of Philadelphia, with every sentiment of respect, gratitude, and esteem," and contain this *Preface :*— " The epithets ' Grotesque ' and ' Arabesque ' will be found to indicate, with sufficient precision, the prevalent tenor of the tales here published. But from the fact that, during a period of some two or three years, I have written five-and-twenty short stories, whose general character may be so briefly defined, it cannot be fairly inferred—at all events it is not truly inferred —that I have for this species of writing any inordinate, or indeed any peculiar, taste or prepossession. I may have written with an eye to this republication in volume form, and may, therefore, have desired to preserve, as far as a certain point, a certain unity of design. This is, indeed, the fact ; and it may even happen that, in this manner, I shall never compose anything again. I speak of these things here, because I am led to think it is the prevalence of the ' Arab-

esque' in my serious tales, which has induced one or
two critics to tax me, in all friendliness, with what
they have been pleased to term 'Germanism' and
gloom. The charge is in bad taste, and the grounds
of the accusation have not been sufficiently considered.
Let us admit, for the moment, that the 'phantasy-
pieces' now given *are* Germanic, or what not. Then
'Germanism' is the vein for the time being. To-mor-
row I may be anything but German, as yesterday I
was everything else. These many pieces are yet one
book. My friends would be quite as wise in taxing
an astronomer with too much astronomy, or an ethical
author with treating too largely of morals. But the
truth is that, with a single exception, there is no one
of these stories in which the scholar should recognise
the distinctive features of that species of pseudo-horror
which we are taught to call Germanic, for no better
reason than some of the secondary names of German
literature have become identified with its folly. If
in many of my productions terror has been the thesis,
I maintain that terror is not of Germany, but of the
soul,—that I have deduced this terror only from its
legitimate sources, and urged it only to its legitimate
results.

" There are one or two of the articles here [conceived
and executed in the purest spirit of extravaganza], to
which I expect no serious attention, and of which I

shall speak no farther. But for the rest I cannot conscientiously claim indulgence on the score of hasty effort. I think it best becomes me to say, therefore, that if I have sinned, I have deliberately sinned. These brief compositions are, in chief part, the results of matured purpose and very careful elaboration."

Besides the tales already referred to in these pages, this two volume collection contains the inferior humoristic pieces, " The man that was used up," " The Devil in the Belfry," " Von Jung "—now known as " Mystification "—and " Why the little Frenchman wears his hand in a sling." This collection does not appear to have received much notice from the press, or to have made any impression upon the public : the edition, which was probably very small, disappeared, and copies of it are of the most extreme rarity.

Among the various publications Poe was now writing for may be mentioned *Alexander's Weekly Messenger*, in which he was airing his theory respecting cryptology, to the effect that human ingenuity could not construct any cryptograph human ingenuity could not decipher. Tested by several correspondents with specimens of their skill in the art of secret writing, the poet actually took the trouble to examine and solve them in triumphant proof, apparently, of the truth of his theory. Another, and scarcely more literary, labour in which he engaged at this time, in

the ceaseless effort " to keep the wolf from the door,"
was the production of a conchological manual for the
use of schools.    Anent this work slander and malice
have said their worst; an enemy, evidently he whose
calumnies, under the guise of " a Memoir," have overclouded the poet's memory ever since his death,
spoke these words in the columns of the Philadelphia
*Saturday Evening Post :*—" One of the most remarkable
plagiarisms was perpetrated by Mr. Poe. . . .    This
gentleman, a few years ago, in Philadelphia, published
a work on Conchology as original, when in reality it
was a copy, nearly verbatim, of ' The Text-Book of
Conchology,' by Captain Thomas Brown, printed in
Glasgow in 1833, a duplicate of which we have in
our library.    Mr. Poe actually took out a copyright
for the American edition of Captain Brown's work,
and, omitting all mention of the English original, pretended, in the preface, to have been under great
obligations to several scientific gentlemen of this city.
It is but justice to add, that in the second edition of
this book, published lately in Philadelphia, the name
of Mr. Poe is withdrawn from the title-page, and his
initials only affixed to the preface.    But the affair is
one of the most curious on record."

Having allowed the slanderer his say, the poet's
own response, *not* included in the above-mentioned
" Memoir," shall be given; but it may be stated that

Poe's work is *not* a plagiarism of Captain Brown's ; that he alluded to obligations to two persons only, one at least of whom, Professor Wyatt, a Scotchman —unaware that the calumny had ever reached Poe's eyes, and not hearing of it himself until ten years after the poet's death—gave an independent, but similar explanatory denial of the accusation in the *Home Journal ;* that Poe's name was *not* withdrawn from the title-page of the second edition, which was called for immediately after the publication of the first, and not after an interval of several years as suggested by the paragraphist.

The poet's letter reads thus :—

"NEW YORK, *Feb.* 16, '47.

"MY DEAR SIR,—Some weeks ago I mailed you two newspapers which, from what you say in your last letter, I see you have not received. I now enclose some slips which will save me the necessity of writing on painful topics. By and by I will write you more at length.

"*Please reinclose the slips when read.*

"What you tell me about the accusation of plagiarism made by the *Phil. Sat. Ev. Post* surprises me. It is the first I heard of it—with the exception of a hint in one of your previous letters—but which I did not then comprehend. Please let me know as many *particulars* as you can remember —for I must see into the charge. Who edits the paper ? who publishes it ? &c. &c. &c. About what time was the accusation made ? I assure you that it is *totally* false. In 1840 I published a book with this title—' The Conchologist's First Book : A system of Testacious Malacology, arranged especially for the use of Schools, in which the animals, *according to Cuvier*, are given with the shells, a great number of new species added, and the whole brought up, as accurately as possible, to the present condition of the science. By Edgar A. Poe. With illustrations of 215 shells, presenting a correct type of each genus.'

" This, I presume, is the work referred to. I wrote it in conjunction with Professor Thomas Wyatt, and Professor McMurtrie, of Philadelphia—my name being put to the work, as best known and most likely to aid its circulation. I wrote the Preface and Introduction, and translated from Cuvier the accounts of the animals, &c. *All* school-books are necessarily made in a similar way. The very title-page acknowledges that the animals are given 'according to Cuvier.' This charge is infamous, and I shall prosecute for it, as soon as I settle my accounts with 'The Mirror.' *
—Truly your friend,                          E. A. POE."

The poet's letter having given the title-page minus only the words, "Published for the Author by Haswell, Barrington, and Haswell," and " Second Edition " added to the title of second issue, it need not be repeated, but the " Prefaces " to the first and second editions are worth recapitulation.  The first is :—

" The term ' Malacology,' an abbreviation of ' Malacozoology,' from the greek μαλαχος, *soft*, ζωον, *an animal*, and λογος, *a discourse*, was first employed by the French naturalist, De

* *Vide* Account of " Action for Libel, Poe *v. Evening Mirror*," vol. ii., p. 113.

Blainville, to designate an important division of Natural History, in which the leading feature of the animals discussed was the *softness* of the flesh, or, to speak with greater accuracy, of the general envelope. This division comprehends not only the *Mollusca*, but also the *Testacea* of Aristotle and of Pliny, and of course, had reference to molluscous animals in general,—of which the greater portion have shells.

"A treatise concerning the shells, exclusively, of this greater portion, is termed, in accordance with general usage, a treatise upon Conchology or Conchyliology ; although the word is somewhat improperly applied, as the Greek *conchylion*, from which it is derived, embraces in its signification both the animal and the shell. Ostracology would have been more definite.

"The common works upon this subject, however, will appear to every person of science very essentially defective, inasmuch as the *relation* of the animal and shell, with their dependence upon each other, is a radically important consideration in the examination of either. Neither in the attempt to obviate this difficulty is a work upon Malacology at large necessarily included. Shells, it is true, form, and, for many obvious reasons, will continue to form, the subject of chief interest, whether with regard to the school or the cabinet; still there is no good reason why a book upon *Conchology* (using the common term) may not be malacological as far as it proceeds.

"In this view of the subject, the present little work is offered to the public. Beyond the ruling feature—that of giving an anatomical account of each animal, together with a description of the shell which it inhabits,—I have aimed at little more than accuracy and simplicity, as far as the latter quality can be thought consistent with the rigid exactions of science.

" No attention has been given to the mere *History* of the subject ; it is conceived that any disquisition on this head would more properly appertain to works of ultimate research, than to one whose sole intention is to make the pupil acquainted, in as tangible a form as possible, with results. To afford, at a cheap rate, a concise, yet a sufficiently comprehensive, and especially a well illustrated school-book, has been the principal design.

" In conclusion, I have only to acknowledge my great indebtedness to the valuable public labours, as well as private assistance, of Mr. Isaac Lea, of Philadelphia. To Mr. Thomas Wyatt, and his excellent *Manual of Conchology*, I am also under many obligations. No better work, perhaps, could be put into the hands of the student as a secondary text-book. Its beautiful and perfectly well-coloured illustrations afford an aid in the collection of a cabinet scarcely to be met with elsewhere. E. A. P."

The Preface to the second edition is :—

" In issuing a second edition of this 'Conchology,' in so very brief a period since the publication of the first large impression, the author has little more to do than to express the high pleasure with which he has seen his labours well received. The success of the work has been decided ; and the entire design has been accomplished in its general introduction into schools.

" Many important alterations and additions are now made ; errors of the press carefully corrected ; and the work, upon the whole, is rendered more worthy of the public approbation. E. A. P."

For the novice, Captain Brown's " Text Book " may

bear some resemblance to Poe's "First Book," from the simple fact that both treatises are founded upon one and the same system; but the absurd charge, that one is, therefore, a plagiarism of the other, can only have been made through gross ignorance or wilful falsehood. As a sequence of these scientific studies, Poe published a translation and digest of Lemonnier's "Natural History," and some other kindred writings.

On the title-page of the *Gentleman's Magazine* for 1840 appear the names of Burton and Poe as joint-editors, although the duties of the former were merely nominal, all the editorial labour devolving upon the poet. For the new volume Poe agreed to write a romance, to be published in serial form, and the first instalment of this story appeared in the January number. "The Journal of Julius Rodman: being an Account of the First Passage across the Rocky Mountains of North America ever achieved by Civilised Man." The projected work was never completed in Burton's Magazine, for reasons that will be seen further on, and its authorship was never hinted at by the various journalists who have published "Memoirs of Poe," until the happy discovery of a letter from the poet to Burton first gave us the clue to its existence. The publication of "Rodman's Journal" in the complete form in which, there is some reason for believing, Poe left the story, would cer-

tainly sustain, if it could not increase, its author's
reputation.   It is written in the realistic manner of
" Arthur Gordon Pym," and although the fragment
at present published breaks off at the moment when
the " Journal " first begins to grow exciting, there is
every probability that the remainder of the work was
calculated to prove of absorbing interest.   The non-
publication in a complete form of the tale was,
doubtless, due to the subsidence of public interest in
exploration of the district to which the " Journal "
refers.   The tale was carried on through the six first
numbers of the *Gentleman's* for 1840, and even in
its present fragmentary state, is well worthy perusal
on account of the idiosyncrastic manner in which
its author identifies himself with his hero—a hero
who suffers from " hereditary hypochondria ; " " was
possessed with a burning love of nature ; and wor-
shipped her, perhaps, more in her dreary and savage
aspects, than in her manifestations of placidity and
joy."   It is unnecessary to furnish an analysis of the
work, but some comments upon it by Mr. William
Sawyer,* one of Poe's staunchest admirers and a poet
himself, are apposite here :—" Without being one of
Poe's most striking, this is certainly one of his most
remarkable works," he observes.   " It displays singular
learning of a varied and exhaustive nature, and is a

* In the London *Mirror* for November 3rd, 1877.

peculiar example of his unique power of giving his fancies the air of reality. Julius Rodman is placed before us as a real flesh-and-blood adventurer, and the early part of the narrative is occupied with details of the preparations for the journey, told to the minutest particular, as if seen to, and set down at the moment by one engaged in making them. The companions of the expedition are all described in detail, so that we seem to live among the persons with whom we are setting out; and after we are once on the journey the incidents, big and little, are recorded day by day as in a log, without literary effort, so that the *vraisemblance* is perfect. . . . The narrative is left unfinished. The Rocky Mountains are not crossed so far as we are permitted to accompany the party, and it is doubtful whether the hand which worked so deftly so far, ever added another line to what would, if carried to completion, have been a work of the type of 'Robinson Crusoe'—a fictitious personal narrative, with the stamp of reality set upon it by the creative power of genius, aided by exceptional capacity for observation and knowledge."

Poe's only other contribution to the *Gentleman's* for January calling for notice, is a review of Moore's "Alciphron." In the course of this critique he advanced the proposition—not a very novel one, perhaps—that the mind of man can *imagine* nothing which has not really existed. Granting, "we can imagine a *griffin*, and that a griffin does not exist," he says in summing up, "not the griffin certainly, but its component parts. It is a mere compendium of known limbs and features—of known qualities. Thus with all that seems to be *new*—which appears to be a *creation* of intellect—it is resolvable into the old. The wildest and most vigorous effort of mind cannot stand the test of this analysis." This same critique also contains Poe's views, in opposition to those of Coleridge, on the suggested difference between *Fancy* and *Imagination*, he citing, as example of the merely fanciful, some lines from "The Culprit Fay"— a then popular American piece—and, as of the loftiest imagination, a piece from Shelley's "Queen Mab."

The February and March issues of the magazine contained little of value by Poe beyond "Rodman's Journal;" there was his sketch, in the former, of "The Business Man"—then headed "Peter Pendulum;"—various odds and ends, and a portion— some being by another hand—of the book notices. These latter included a review of Longfellow's "Voices of the Night," in which, whilst awarding his countryman very high praise as a poet, he charged him with plagiarising the conception of "The Midnight Mass for the Dying Year" from Tennyson's "Death of the Old Year." Beyond instalments of "Rodman's Jour-

nal," the April and May numbers did not contain much
noticeable writing by Poe, but the former included
"Silence: a sonnet," with the burden of "No more"
—the germ of a refrain to be so famous hereafter—
and the latter a critique on Bryant, and an essay
on "The Philosophy of Furniture." The last sketch
was subsequently revised and enlarged, but even then
portrayed its author's artistic love of the luxurious and
beautiful. With the June number the *Gentleman's
Magazine* passed from Mr. Burton's hands into the
possession of Mr. George R. Graham, and, at the same
time, Edgar Poe's editorial duties came to an end.
The following letter from the poet to Mr. Burton will
throw some light upon the affair :—

"Sir,—I find myself at leisure this Monday morning,
June 1, to notice your very singular letter of Saturday. . . .
I have followed the example of Victorine and slept upon the
matter, and you shall now hear what I have to say.  In the
first place, your attempts to bully me excite in my mind
scarcely any other sentiment than mirth.  When you address
me again preserve, if you can, the dignity of a gentleman. . .
I shall feel myself more at liberty to be explicit.  As for the
rest, you do me gross injustice ; and you know it.  As usual,
you have wrought yourself into a passion with me on account
of some imaginary wrong; for no real injury, or attempt at
injury, have you ever received at my hands.  As I live, I am
utterly unable to say why you are angry, or what true grounds
of complaint you have against me.  You are a man of impulses ; have made yourself, in consequence, some enemies ;

have been in many respects ill-treated by those whom you had looked upon as friends—and these things have rendered you suspicious. You once wrote in your magazine a sharp critique upon a book of mine—a very silly book—Pym. Had I written a similar criticism upon a book of yours, you feel that you would have been my enemy for life, and you therefore imagine in my bosom a latent hostility towards yourself. This has been a mainspring in your whole conduct towards me since our first acquaintance. It has acted to prevent all cordiality. In a general view of human nature your idea is just—but you will find yourself puzzled in judging me by ordinary motives. Your criticism was essentially correct, and therefore, although severe, it did not occasion in me one solitary emotion either of anger or dislike. But even while I write these words, I am sure you will not believe them. Did I not still think you, in spite of the exceeding littleness of some of your hurried actions, a man of many honorable impulses, I should not now take the trouble to send you this letter. I cannot permit myself to suppose that you would say to me in cool blood what you said in your letter of yesterday. You are, of course, only mistaken, in asserting that I owe you a hundred dollars, and you will rectify the mistake at once when you come to look at your accounts.

Soon after I joined you, you made me an offer of money, and I accepted $20. Upon another occasion, at my request, you sent me enclosed in a letter $30. Of this 30, I repaid 20 within the next fortnight (drawing no salary for that period). I was thus still in your debt $30, when not long ago I again asked a loan of $30, which you promptly handed to me at your own house. Within the last three weeks, three dollars each week have been retained from my salary, an indignity which I have felt deeply but did not resent. You state the sum retained as $8, but this I believe is through a mistake of Mr. Morrell. My postage bill, at a guess, might be $9 or $10—and I therefore am indebted to you, upon the whole, in the amount of about $60. More than this sum I shall not pay. You state that you can no longer afford to pay $50 per month for 2 or 3 pp. of MS. Your error here can be shown by reference to the Magazine. During my year with you I have written—

| | | | | |
|---|---|---|---|---|
| In July | 5 | pp. | | |
| ,, August | 9 | ,, | | |
| ,, Sept. | 16 | ,, | | |
| ,, Oct. | 4 | ,, | | |
| ,, Nov. | 5 | ,, | | |
| ,, Dec. | 12 | ,, | | |
| ,, Jan. | 9 | ,, | | |
| ,, Feb. | 12 | ,, | | |
| ,, March | 11 | ,, | | |
| ,, April | 17 | ,, | | |
| ,, May | 14 | ,, | + 5 copied—Miss McMichael's MS. |
| ,, June | 9 | ,, | + 3 ,, | Chandlers. |

132 (*sic*)

"Dividing this sum by 12, we have an average of 11 pp. per month—not 2 or 3. And this estimate leaves out of question everything in the way of extract or compilation. Nothing is counted but *bonâ fide* composition. 11 pp. at $3 per p. would be $33, at the usual Magazine prices. Deduct this from $50, my monthly salary, and we have left $17 per month, or $4 $\frac{25}{100}$ per week, for the services of proof-reading; general superintendence at the printing office; reading, altera- tion, and preparation of MSS., with compilation of various articles, such as Plate articles, Field Sports, &c. Neither has anything been said of my name upon your title-page, a small

item, you will say — but still something, as you know.
Snowden pays his editresses $2 per week each for their
names *solely*. Upon the whole, I am not willing to admit
that you have greatly overpaid me. That I did not do four
times as much as I did for the Magazine was your own fault.
At first I wrote long articles, which you deemed inadmissible,
and never did I suggest any to which you had not some immediate and decided objection. Of course I grew discouraged,
and could feel no interest in the journal.

"I am at a loss to know why you call me selfish. If you
mean that I borrowed money of you—you know that you
offered it, and you know that I am poor. In what instance
has any one ever found me selfish? Was there selfishness
in the affront I offered Benjamin (whom I respect, and who
spoke well of me) because I deemed it a duty not to receive
from any one commendation at your expense? . . . I have said
that I could not tell why you were angry. Place yourself in
my situation, and see whether you would not have acted as I
have done. You first 'enforced,' as you say, a deduction of
salary : giving me to understand thereby that you thought of
parting company. You next spoke disrespectfully of me behind my back—this as an habitual thing—to those whom you
supposed your friends, and who punctually retailed me, as a
matter of course, every ill-natured word which you uttered.
Lastly, you advertised your magazine for sale without saying
a word to me about it. I felt no anger at what you did—
none in the world. Had I not firmly believed it your design
to give up your journal, with a view of attending to the
Theatre, I should never have dreamed of attempting one of
my own. The opportunity of doing something for myself
seemed a good one—(and I was about to be thrown out of
business)—and I embraced it. Now I ask you, as a man of

honor and as a man of sense—what is there wrong in all
this ?  What have I done at which you have any right to
take offence ?  I can give you no definitive answer (respecting
the continuation of Rodman's Journal) until I hear from you
again.  The charge of $100 I shall not admit for an instant.
If you persist in it our intercourse is at an end, and we can
each adopt our own measures.

" In the meantime, I am,

" Yr. Obt. St.,

" EDGAR A. POE.

" WM. E. BURTON, Esq."

Whatever soreness there may have been at this
time between the co-editors, it appears to have ultimately worn away, for Poe spoke in friendly terms
of Burton in his subsequent papers on " Autography,"
and Burton wrote defending the poet when, upon his
decease, his character was assailed.  Doubtless an
amicable arrangement was subsequently arrived at,
and, in all probability, Poe repaid his indebtedness—
set forth in this letter with all his habitual careful-
ness—by a certain amount of " copy " to be used, and
which was used, apparently, in the magazine after it
passed out of the possession of its founder into the
hands of Mr. Graham.

After his severance from the *Gentleman's,* Poe
endeavoured to found a new monthly journal of his
own, to be called the *Penn Magazine,* but the project
fell through after the prospectus had been circulated

among the members of the publishing world. The chief wording of this prospectus was subsequently adopted for the basis of a later project, to be adverted to hereafter, and need not, therefore, be cited from. Want of the necessary funds, and inability to secure a sufficient number of subscribers doubtless caused the failure of the poet's scheme.

## CHAPTER XII.

*EDITOR OF GRAHAM'S MAGAZINE.*

FOR the five months following Poe's secession, nothing of his of any consequence appeared in the *Gentleman's Magazine.* The purchaser, Mr. Graham, was not only a man of literary proclivities but also a shrewd man of business, and he speedily recognised the value of the ex-editor's services. In November, therefore, he arranged with Poe to resume his former post on the magazine, which from the beginning of the forthcoming new year was to be amalgamated with another periodical styled the *Casket,* and henceforward was to be known as *Graham's Magazine.* To the last—the December—number of the *Gentleman's,* Poe contributed his gruesome sketch, "The Man of the Crowd." This weird record of the solitude-dreading mortal—this impersonation of La Bruyere's "*grand malheur de ne pouvoir être seul*"—appeals more strongly to the human heart than any of its author's other prose works, the majority of which, as is so generally acknowledged, subdue the intellect only. What a fascination for the thoughtful, whose thinking is prompted by heart as well as brain, lurks in these opening sentences of the tale !

" It was well said of a certain German book that ' *es läszt sich nicht lesen* '—it does not permit itself to be read.    There are some secrets which do not permit themselves to be. told.    Men die nightly in their beds, wringing the hands of ghostly confessors, and looking them piteously in the eyes, die with despair of heart and convulsion in throat, on account of the hideous-ness of mysteries which will not *suffer themselves* to be revealed.    Now and then, alas, the conscience of man takes up a burthen so heavy in horror that it can be thrown down only into the grave.    And thus the essence of all crime is undivulged."

The description of a convalescent's feelings of serene contentment in the return of health, when he finds himself " in one of those happy moods which are so precisely the converse of *ennui*—moods of the keenest appetency, when the film from the mental vision departs," is a faithful portrayal of the experience of many, and is, therefore, widely different from Poe's usual psychological observations, which are mostly based upon the *outrè* and the abnormal.    " The Man of the Crowd " stands forth as a specimen of its author's real genius—his masterly powers of combined suggestiveness and description.

From the beginning of 1841, and for some time

henceforward, the history of Edgar Poe is merged into, and becomes chiefly, the recital of his literary labours, the most remarkable of which now consisted of contributions to *Graham's Magazine.* The worthy proprietor of that publication speedily received due reward for his appreciation of Poe's talents. Indeed, it is declared that in a little less than two years the number of subscribers to the magazine increased from five to fifty-two thousand, and this, although aided by Mr. Graham's liberality to his contributors, was mainly due to the new editor. His daring critiques, his analytic essays, and his weird stories, following one another in rapid succession, startled the public, and compelled it to an acknowledgment of his powers. New enemies were created, however, by the dauntless intrepidity with which he assailed the fragile reputations of the small bookmakers, especially in his pungent papers on "Autography."

In the April number of *Graham's* appeared Poe's world-famed story of "The Murders in the Rue Morgue." It was the first of a series—the series aptly termed by Baudelaire, "*une espéce de trilogie*"—illustrative of an analytic phase of its author's complex mind. The particular idiosyncrasy in which the tale germinated is thus introduced in the exordium :—

" The mental features discoursed of as the analytical are, in themselves, but little susceptible of analysis. We appreciate them only in their effects.  We know of them, among other things, that they are always to their possessor, when inordinately possessed, a source of the liveliest enjoyment.  As the strong man exults in his physical ability, delighting in such exercises as call his muscles into action, so glories the analyst in that moral activity which *disentangles.*  He derives pleasure from even the most trivial occupations bringing his talent into play.  He is fond of enigmas, of conundrums, of hieroglyphics ; exhibiting in his solutions of each a degree of *acumen* which appears to the ordinary apprehension preternatural.  His results, brought about by the very soul and essence of method, have, in truth, the whole air of intuition.

"The faculty of re-solution is possibly much invigorated by mathematical study, and especially by that highest branch of it which, unjustly, and merely on account of its retrograde operations, has been called, as if *par excellence,* analysis. Yet to calculate is not in itself to analyse.  A chess-player, for example, does the one without effort at the other.  It follows that the game of chess, in its effects upon mental character, is greatly misunderstood. . . .  I will, therefore, take occasion to assert that the higher powers of the reflective intellect are more decidedly and more usefully tasked by the unostentatious game of draughts than by all the elaborate frivolity of chess.  In this latter, where the pieces have different and *bizarre* motions, with various and variable values, what is only complex is mistaken (a not unusual error) for what is profound.  The *attention* is here called powerfully into play.  If it flag for an instant, an oversight is committed, resulting in injury or defeat.  The possible moves being not only manifold but involute, the chances of such oversights are multiplied ; and in nine cases out of ten it is

the more concentrative rather than the more acute player who
conquers. In draughts, on the contrary, where the moves
are *unique* and have but little variation, the probabilities of
inadvertence are diminished, and the mere attention being
left comparatively unemployed, what advantages are obtained
by either party are obtained by superior *acumen.* To be less
abstract—let us suppose a game of draughts where the
pieces are reduced to four kings, and where, of course, no
oversight is to be expected. It is obvious that here the vic-
tory can be decided (the players being at all equal) only by
some *recherché* movement, the result of some strong exertion
of the intellect. Deprived of ordinary resources, the analyst
throws himself into the spirit of his opponent, identifies
himself therewith, and not unfrequently sees thus, at a
glance, the sole methods (sometimes indeed absurdly simple
ones) by which he may seduce into error or hurry into mis-
calculation.

"Whist has long been noted for its influence upon what
is termed the calculating power; and men of the highest
order of intellect have been known to take an apparently
unaccountable delight in it, while eschewing chess as frivo-
lous. Beyond doubt there is nothing of a similar nature so
greatly tasking the faculty of analysis. The best chess-
player in Christendom *may* be little more than the best
player of chess; but proficiency in whist implies capacity
for success in all those more important undertakings where
mind struggles with mind. When I say proficiency, I mean
that perfection in the game which includes a comprehension
of *all* the sources whence legitimate advantage may be derived. These are not only manifold but multiform, and lie
frequently among recesses of thought altogether inaccessible
to the ordinary understanding. To observe attentively is

to remember distinctly ; and, so far, the concentrative chess-
player will do very well at whist ; while the rules of Hoyle
(themselves based upon the mere mechanism of the game)
are sufficiently and generally comprehensible.   Thus to have
a retentive memory, and to proceed by 'the book,' are
points commonly regarded as the sum total of good playing.
But it is in matters beyond the limits of mere rule that the
skill of the analyst is evinced.   He makes, in silence, a host
of observations and inferences.   So, perhaps, do his companions ; and the difference in the extent of the.information
obtained lies not so much in the validity of the inference
as in the quality of the observation.   .The necessary knowledge is that of *what* to observe.   Our player confines
himself not at all ; nor, because the game is the object, does
he reject deductions from things external to the game.   He
examines the countenance of his partner, comparing it carefully with that of each of his opponents.   He considers the
mode of assorting the cards in each hand ; often counting
trump by trump, and honour by honour, through the glances
bestowed by their holders upon each.   He notes every variation of face as the play progresses, gathering a fund of
thought from the differences in the expression of certainty,
of surprise, of triumph, or of chagrin.   From the manner of
gathering up a trick he judges whether the person taking it
can make another in the suit.   He recognises what is played
through feint, by the air with which it is thrown upon the
table.   A casual or inadvertent word ; the accidental drop-
ping or turning of a card, with the accompanying anxiety
or carelessness in regard to its concealment ; the counting
of the tricks, with the order of their arrangement ; embarrassment, hesitation, eagerness or trepidation—all afford, to
his apparently intuitive perception, indications of the true

state of affairs. The first two or three rounds having been played, he is in full possession of the contents of each hand, and thenceforward puts down his cards with as absolute a precision of purpose as if the rest of the party had turned outward the faces of their own.

"The analytical power should not be confounded with simple ingenuity; for while the analyst is necessarily ingenious, the ingenious man is often remarkably incapable of analysis. The constructive or combining power, by which ingenuity is usually manifested, and to which the phrenologists (I believe erroneously) have assigned a separate organ, supposing it a primitive faculty, has been so frequently seen in those whose intellect bordered otherwise upon idiocy, as to have attracted general observation among writers on morals. Between ingenuity and the analytic ability there exists a difference far greater indeed than that between the fancy and the imagination, but of a character very strictly analogous. It will be found, in fact, that the ingenious are always fanciful, and the *truly* imaginative never otherwise than analytic."

" The Murders in the Rue Morgue " (as also the two narratives in a similar strain which shortly followed), are desired by their author to be read somewhat in the light of commentaries upon the propositions advanced in the preceding remarks. Accepted as fiction merely, their merit is pre-eminently conspicuous, but as demonstrations of the mental problems to which they refer, they deserve the earnest attention of the psychologist and moral philosopher, and entitle Poe's works to study in quarters where the productions of the mere romancist are rarely or never known.

Poe's name was first introduced to the French public by " The Murders in the Rue Morgue," the tale, shortly after its appearance in *Graham's*, being copied with complimentary comment into the Paris *Charivari*, the translator objecting, however, that no such street as the *Rue Morgue* existed ("so far as he knew," says Poe) in Paris. This circumstance was also cited in after years by Baudelaire as one of a series of proofs that the poet had never visited the French metropolis ! Some years later the tale reappeared in *Le Commerce*, as an original *feuilleton*, under the title of " L'Orang-Otang," and shortly afterwards *La Quotidienne*, aware, apparently, of the source whence the work had been obtained, transferred it bodily to its own columns. This being noticed by a third journal as a case of gross plagiarism, a lawsuit was instituted, during the hearing of which *Le Commerce* proved that Edgar Poe was the real and sole author of the story in question. The interest created by this legal inquiry induced Madame Isabella Meunier to translate several of Poe's tales for the *Democratic Pacifique* and other French journals.

In the May number of *Graham's* appeared another of Poe's prose *chefs d'œuvre*, the weird narrative entitled " A Descent into the Maelström." Scientific truth and poetic invention have never been more artistically blended than in this most marvellous and idiosyncratic tale : its author having learned the natural secret that a cylindrical body, revolving in a vortex, offers more resistance to its suction, and is consequently drawn into it with greater difficulty than bodies of any other form of equal bulk, instead of inditing a chapter on mechanics, charms all readers with a story of weird and fascinating power.

On the first of the same month he contributed to the Philadelphia *Saturday Evening Post*—a paper belonging to Mr. Graham, and for which Poe wrote critiques—another startling manifestation of his analytic capabilities, in a *prospective* review of Dickens's story of "Barnaby Rudge." In this review the poet explained with mathematical exactitude what should be the plot of the as-yet-unwritten story, and the correctness of his solution drew from Dickens a letter of flattering acknowledgment, in which he inquired whether Mr. Poe had dealings with the devil. Alluding to the poet's wonderful analysis of his plot, Dickens says, " By the way, are you aware that Godwin wrote his ' Caleb Williams ' backwards ? He first involved his hero in a web of difficulties, forming the second volume, and then, for the first, cast about him for some mode of accounting for what had been done." Some years later, Poe, commenting upon this remark, after noting that this was not the *precise* mode of procedure on Godwin's part, says, " But the author of ' Caleb Williams ' was too good an artist not to perceive the advantage derivable from at least a somewhat similar process," a process, indeed, not altogether divergent from Poe's own acknowledged method of retaining the *dénouement* of his work always before him, and subordinating all incident, tone, even verbal combination, to the development of this idea. But for deficiency in construction of plot he criticised the author of " Pickwick," deeming that he had no positive *genius* for *adaptation*, and still less, in Poe's judgment, " for that metaphysical art in which the souls of all *mysteries* lie," yet apart from this drawback, he expressed an intense reverence for Dickens, deeming him England's greatest living novelist.

In the July number of *Graham's* Poe reverted to his favourite theme of cryptography, in an article styled " A few Words on Secret Writing." It was a subject to which he had already devoted some time, both at home and in the papers of New York and Philadelphia, and this magazine article was the result of, and in connection with, his challenges to the public to produce a cryptographic riddle he should not be able to resolve. " The facility with which he would unravel the most dark and perplexing ciphers," writes a clerical friend, " was really supernatural. Out of a

most confused medley of letters, figures, and cabalistic
characters, in any of the seven different languages,
the English, German, French, Spanish, Italian, Latin
and Greek, his wonderful power of analysis would,
almost at once, evolve sense, order, and beauty; and of
the hundreds of cryptographs which he received while
editor of one of our popular periodicals, he never failed
to solve one unless it was illegitimate, that is, unless
its author put it together not intending to have it
made sense. During a visit which he paid to Lowell,
designing to test his cryptographical skill, I wrote a
short paragraph somewhat in the following fashion.*
. . . The sentence was this :—

"'The patient was severely attacked with spasms
and acute pain in the hypogastric region; remedial
agents were employed; but without effect, and death
soon ensued.' This rendered into cipher in the manner
shown * above would be :— 'Gurengvragjuffrireryl
nggnpxrgjigufonfzfnaqnqhgrcnvavagurulcbtnfgevpertvb
aerzrqrnyntragfjrerrzcybirqohgjigubhgrssrpgnaqqrngufb
bararafirq.'

"Mr. Poe solved this cipher in one-fifth of the time
it took me to write it. This, however, is one of the
most simple forms of cryptography."

In his magazine article, Poe deemed it scarcely possible to "imagine a time when there did not exist a

* The process need not be described in these pages.—J. H. I.

necessity, or at least a desire, of transmitting information from one individual to another in such manner as to elude general comprehension," and, whilst tracing the history of the art of secret writing from dim antiquity, he propounds the dictum, that " means of secret intercommunication must have existed almost contemporaneously with the invention of letters." Further dilating upon the congenial theme, he says:—

" Few persons can be made to believe that it is not quite an easy thing to invent a method of secret writing which shall baffle investigation. Yet it may be roundly asserted that human ingenuity cannot concoct a cipher which human ingenuity cannot resolve. In the facility with which such writing is deciphered, however, there exist very remarkable differences in different intellects. Often, in the case of two individuals of acknowledged equality as regards ordinary mental efforts, it will be found that, while one cannot unriddle the commonest cipher, the other will scarcely be puzzled by the most abstruse. It may be observed generally that in such investigations the analytic ability is very forcibly called into action ; and, for this reason, cryptographical solutions might with great propriety be introduced into academies as the means of giving tone to the most important of the powers of mind. . . .

" At a cursory glance, these various modes of constructing a cipher seem to have about them an air of inscrutable secrecy. It appears almost an impossibility to unriddle what has been put together by so complex a method. And to some persons the difficulty might be great ; but to others —to those skilled in deciphering—such enigmas are very simple indeed. The reader should bear in mind that the basis of the whole art of solution, as far as regards these matters, is found in the general principles of the formation of language itself, and thus is altogether independent of the particular laws which govern any cipher, or the construction of its key. The difficulty of reading a cryptographical puzzle is by no means always in accordance with the labour or ingenuity with which it has been constructed. The sole use of the key, indeed, is for those *au fait* to the cipher; in its perusal by a third party, no reference is had to it at all. The lock of the secret is picked. In the different methods of cryptography specified above,* it will be observed that there is a gradually increasing complexity. But this complexity is only in shadow. It has no substance whatever. It appertains merely to the formation, and has no bearing upon the solution of the cipher. The last mode mentioned is not in the least degree more difficult to be deciphered than the first, whatever may be the difficulty of either."

Some amusing incidents growing out of Poe's dealings with cryptology are thus reverted to:—

"In the discussion of an analogous subject, in one of the weekly papers † of this city, about eighteen months ago, the writer of this article had occasion to speak of the application of a rigorous *method* in all forms of thought — of its advantages — of the extension of its use even to what is considered the operation of pure fancy — and thus, subsequently, of the solution of cipher. He even ventured to assert that no cipher, of the character above specified,

---

* In *Graham's Magazine.*—J. H. I.
† Philadelphia *Saturday Evening Post.*—J. H. I.

could be sent to the address of the paper, which he would
not be able to resolve. This challenge excited, most unex-
pectedly, a very lively interest among the numerous readers
of the journal. Letters were poured in upon the editor
from all parts of the country; and many of the writers of
these epistles were so convinced of the impenetrability of
their mysteries, as to be at great pains to draw him into
wagers on the subject. At the same time, they were not
always scrupulous about sticking to the point. The cryptographs were, in numerous instances, altogether beyond the
limits defined in the beginning. Foreign languages were
employed. Words and sentences were run together without interval. Several alphabets were used in the same
cipher. One gentleman, but moderately endowed with
conscientiousness, inditing us a puzzle composed of pot-
hooks and hangers to which the wildest typography of the
office could afford nothing similar, went even so far as to
jumble together no less than *seven distinct alphabets*, without
intervals between the letters *or between the lines*. Many of
the cryptographs were dated in Philadelphia, and several
of those which urged the subject of a bet were written by
gentlemen of this city. Out of, perhaps, one hundred
ciphers altogether received, there was only one which we
did not immediately succeed in resolving. This one we
*demonstrated* to be an imposition; that is to say, we fully
proved it a jargon of random characters, having no meaning whatever. In respect to the epistle of the seven
alphabets, we had the pleasure of completely *nonpluss*-ing its
inditer by a prompt and satisfactory translation.

"The weekly paper mentioned was, for a period of some
months, greatly occupied with the hieroglyphic and caba-
listic-looking solutions of the cryptographs sent us from all

quarters. Yet, with the exception of the writers of the
ciphers, we do not believe that any individuals could have
been found among the readers of the journal who regarded
the matter in any other light than in that of a desperate
humbug. We mean to say that no one really believed in
the authenticity of the answers. One party averred that
the mysterious figures were only inserted to give a *queer*
air to the paper, for the purpose of attracting attention.
Another thought it more probable that we not only solved
the ciphers, but put them together ourselves for solution.
This having been the state of affairs at the period when it
was thought expedient to decline further dealings in necromancy, the writer of this article avails himself of the present opportunity to maintain the truth of the journal in
question—to repel the charges of rigmarole by which it was
assailed—and to declare, in his own name, that the ciphers
were all written in good faith, and solved in the same spirit."

The interest and excitement created by this public
discussion on secret writing continually increased; and
Poe, not liking to be conquered, continually wasted
valuable time and labour on the, to him, unprofitable
occupation of correspondence there anent, until, in the
August number of *Graham's Magazine*, the following
correspondence and comments commenced :—

"Just as we were going to press with the last sheet of
this number," writes the editor, "we received the following
letter from the well-known author of 'Clinton Bradshawe,'
'Howard Pinckney,' &c., &c. :—

"'My Dear Sir,—The enclosed cryptograph is from a
friend of mine [Dr. Frailey], who thinks he can puzzle you.

If you decipher it, then you are a magician ; for he has used,
as I think, the greatest art in making it.—Your friend,

' F. W. Thomas.'"

There is no necessity to cite the intricate puzzle
which followed this note, in reply to which Poe said :
" By return of mail we sent the solution to Mr. Thomas ;
but as the cipher is an exceedingly ingenious one, we
forbear publishing its translation here, and prefer
testing the ability of our readers to solve it. *We will
give a year's subscription to the magazine, and also a
year's subscription to the "Saturday Evening Post," to any
person, or rather to the first person, who shall read us
this riddle.* We have no expectation that it will be
read ; and therefore, should the month pass without
an answer forthcoming, we will furnish the key to the
cipher, and again offer a year's subscription to the
magazine, to any person—who shall solve it *with the
key.*" To this Poe appended the statement that, in
the magazine, he had only undertaken to decipher a
certain class of cryptographs, and to this limit he must
hold his correspondents, adding, " To be sure, we said
that 'human ingenuity could not construct a cipher
which human ingenuity could not resolve ;' but then
we do not propose, just now, to make ourselves individ-
ually the test of 'human ingenuity' in general. We
do not propose to solve *all* ciphers. Whether we can
or cannot do this is a question for another day—a

day when we have more leisure than at present we have any hope of enjoying. The most simple cryptograph requires, in its solution, labour, patience, and much time. We therefore abide by the limits of our cartel. It is true that in attempting the perusal of Dr. Frailey's we have exceeded these limits by very much; but we were seduced into the endeavour to read it by the decided manner in which an opinion was expressed that we could not."

Of *Graham's* many thousands of readers none had solved the puzzle by the time stated; its solution was, therefore, furnished in the October number, together with a letter from Dr. Frailey of Washington, as an evidence not only of its correctness but also of its attendant difficulties, not that such proof seemed requisite, after the failure of the public to decipher the enigma. It will be seen that, in order to increase the embarrassment of the would-be elucidator, the doctor had used arbitrary characters to represent *whole words*, which, taken in connection with the other difficulties mentioned in his note, and the extraordinary phraseology employed, enables us to better appreciate the work accomplished :—

" WASHINGTON, *July 6,* 1841.

"DEAR SIR,—It gives me pleasure to state that the reading by Mr. Poe, of the cryptograph which I gave you a few days since for transmission to him, is correct.

"I am the more astonished at this, since for various words of two, three, and four letters, a distinct character was used for each, in order to prevent the discovery of some of those words, by their frequent repetition in a cryptograph of any length, and applying them to other words. I also used a distinct character for the terminations *tion* and *sion*, and substituted in every word where it was possible, some of the characters above alluded to. Where the same word of two of those letters occurred frequently, the letters of the key-phrase and the characters were alternately used, to increase the difficulty.—As ever, yours, &c.,    CHARLES S. FRAILEY.

"To F. W. THOMAS, Esq."

This note from the propounder of the cryptograph was enclosed in the following letter from Poe's friend, Thomas :—

"WASHINGTON, *July* 6, 1841.

"MY DEAR SIR, This morning I received yours of yesterday, deciphering the 'cryptograph' which I sent you last week from my friend, Doctor Frailey. You request that I would obtain the Doctor's acknowledgment of your solution ; I have just received the enclosed from him.

"Doctor Frailey had heard me speak of your having deciphered a letter which our mutual friend, Dow, wrote upon a challenge from you last year, at my lodgings in your city, when Aaron Burr's correspondence in cipher was the subject of our conversation. You laughed at what you termed Burr's shallow artifice, and said you could decipher any such cryptography easily. To test you on the spot, Dow withdrew to the corner of the room, and wrote a letter in cipher, which you solved in a much shorter time than it took him to indite it.

"As Doctor Frailey seemed to doubt your skill to the extent of my belief in it, when your article on 'Secret Writing' appeared in the last number of your Magazine, I showed it to him. After reading it, he remarked that he thought he could puzzle you, and the next day he handed me the cryptograph which I transmitted to you. He did not tell me the key. The uncommon nature of his article, of which I gave you not the slightest hint, made me express to you my strong doubts of your ability to make the solution. I confess that your solution, so speedily and correctly made, surprised me. I congratulate myself that I do not live in an age when the black art is believed in, for, innocent as I am of all knowledge of cryptography, I should be arrested as an accessory before the fact, and, though I escaped, it is certain that you would have to die the death, and, alas! I fear upon my testimony. Your friend,                                        F. W. THOMAS.

"EDGAR A. POE, Esq."

A transcript of the "solution" will afford an idea of some of the difficulties to be overcome in its discovery :—

"In one of those peripatetic circumrotations I obviated a rustic whom I subjected to catechetical interrogation respecting the nosocomical characteristics of the edifice to which I was approximate. With a volubility uncongealed by the frigorific powers of villatic bashfulness, he ejaculated a voluminous replication from the universal tenor of whose contents I deduce the subsequent amalgamation of heterogeneous facts. Without dubiety incipient pretension is apt to terminate in final vulgarity, as parturient mountains have been fabulated to produce muscupular abortions. The institution the subject of my remarks, has not been without cause the theme of the ephemeral columns of quotidian journals, and enthusiastic encomiations in conversational intercourse."

The key to this cipher is as follows:—" *But find this out, and I give it up.*"

Poe was not permitted to drop this subject so readily as he desired, at least as regards publicity.    In publishing a long letter, in the December number of *Graham's*, from a Mr. Tyler—who stated that he had been practically conversant with secret writing for several years, and must admit that, in the solution of the intricate hieroglyphics submitted to him, Poe had exhibited a power of analytical and synthetical reasoning he had never seen equalled — the poet, whilst commenting upon several misapprehensions in his correspondent's communication, pointed out that his time was much occupied; and as, notwithstanding the limits he had originally assigned to the challenged, they still continued to overwhelm him with correspondence, he must, perforce, in future decline to say anything further on the subject, deeply interesting though he found it to be.

Meanwhile, in addition to this cryptographic matter, and the strain of editorial duties, Poe was also contributing reviews and book notices to the monthly issues of *Graham's Magazine;* in July, amongst other matters, was a very eulogistic critique on Bolingbroke,

and some remarkable utterances on the Temperance
Movement. This latter, Poe declared, was the most
important reformation the world had ever known, but
that "its *great* feature had never yet been made a
subject of comment. We mean," he explained, "that
of adding to man's happiness . . . by the simple and
most effectual process of exalting his capacity for
enjoyment. The temperate man," he opined, " carries
within his own bosom, under all circumstances, the
true, the only elements of bliss."

The weird "Colloquy of Monos and Una," already
alluded to in connection with the Stannard episode, appeared in the August number of *Graham's*.
This tale, in its attempt to search out the secrets
of mortality *beyond death*—to define the indefinable
—is most masterful; nor Coleridge, nor De Quincey,
nor any man, ever wrought the like; and, as a literary work, it is simply unique. The early portion
of the " Colloquy " is an attack upon certain utili-
tarian and democratic tendencies of the time, the
value and ultimate results of which were by no
means perceptible to the poet. " At long intervals,"
one of his ultra-mortal characters remarks, "some
master-minds appeared, looking upon each advance in
practical science as a retrogradation in the true utility;
. . . that knowledge was not meet for man in the
infant condition of his soul. . . . The poets—living

and perishing amid the scorn of the ' utilitarians '—
of rough pedants, who arrogated to themselves a title
which could have been properly applied only to the
scorned—these men, the poets, pondered piningly, yet
not unwisely, upon the ancient days when our wants
were not more simple than our enjoyments were keen ;
—days when *mirth* was a word unknown, so solemnly
deep-toned was happiness ;—holy, august, and blissful
days, when blue rivers ran undammed, between hills
unknown, into far-forest solitudes, primeval, odorous,
and unexplored. . . . Alas! we had fallen upon the
most evil of all our evil days. The great ' movement '—that was the cant term—went on : a dis-
eased commotion, moral and physical. . . . Among
other odd ideas, that of universal equality gained
ground ; and in the face of analogy and of God—
in despite of the loud warning voice of the laws of
*gradation* so visibly pervading all things — wild
attempts at an omniprevalent democracy were made."
From this vain and vague outbreak at the nature of
surrounding things, the poet passes on to the true theme
of his imagination, to that strange attempt to pierce
the impenetrable veil which overshrouds the visage of
death made in this " Colloquy."

The same month that this tale appeared, appeared
also several reviews by Poe. In the most important
of these, that on Mr. Wilmer's " Quacks of Helicon,"

the poet's discontent at the contemporary state of
affairs is strongly expressed, and it is easy to comprehend, after perusal of this philippic, why certain
members of the American literary republic are still
so sore when Poe or Wilmer are on the *tapis.* The
former welcomes the work under review because,
.among other reasons, " in the universal corruption and
rigmarole amid which we gasp for breath, it is really
a pleasant thing to get even one accidental whiff of
the unadulterated air of *truth.*" The reviewer, after
reprimanding Mr. Wilmer for the indecency of his
satire, which he considers has done the work irre-
parable injury, without in any way enhancing its
value on the score of sarcasm, vigour, or wit, as
nothing vulgar should "*ever* be said or conceived,"
proceeds to commend the author for, above all his
other merits, the far loftier merit of speaking fear-
lessly the truth, at an epoch when truth is out of
fashion, and under circumstances of social position
which would have deterred almost any man in our
community from a similar Quixotism. "For the publication of the 'Quacks of Helicon,'—a poem which
brings under review, by name, most of our prominent
*literati*, and treats them, generally, as they deserve
(what treatment could be more bitter ?)—for the
publication of this attack, Mr. Wilmer, whose subsistence lies in his pen, has little to look for—apart

from the silent respect of those at once honest and
timid—but the most malignant open or covert per-
secution.  For this reason, and because it is the truth
which he has spoken, do we say to him from the
bottom of our hearts, God speed ! "

"We repeat it : *it is* the truth which he has spoken ;
and who shall contradict us ?  He has said unscrupulously
what every reasonable man among us has long known to be
' as true as the Pentateuch '—that, as a literary people, we
are one vast perambulating humbug.  He has asserted that
we are *clique*-ridden ; and who does not smile at the obvious
truism of that assertion ?  He maintains that chicanery is,
with us, a far surer road than talent to distinction in letters.
Who gainsays this ?  The corrupt nature of our ordinary
criticism has become notorious.  Its powers have been pros-
trated by its own arm.  The intercourse between critic and
publisher, as it now almost universally stands, is comprised
either in the paying and pocketing of black-mail, as the price
of a simple forbearance, or in a direct system of petty and
contemptible bribery, properly so called—a system even more
injurious than the former to the true interests of the public,
and more degrading to the buyers and sellers of good opinion,
on account of the more positive character of the service here
rendered for the consideration received.  We laugh at the
idea of any denial of our assertions upon this topic ; they are
infamously true.  In the charge of general corruption, there
are undoubtedly many noble exceptions to be made.  There
are, indeed, some very few editors, who, maintaining an entire
independence, will receive no books from publishers at all, or
who receive them with a perfect understanding, on the part
of these latter, that an unbiassed *critique* will be given.  But

these cases are insufficient to have much effect on the popular mistrust : a mistrust heightened by late exposure of the machinations of *coteries* in New York—*coteries* which, at the bidding of leading booksellers, manufacture, as required from time to time, a pseudo-public opinion by wholesale, for the benefit of any little hanger-on of the party, or pettifogging protector of the firm."

It is impossible to avoid sympathising with Poe's scornful bitterness, in respect to this matter, and to help feeling that the existing evil—for the evil did exist then, and does exist now—could only be met by such outspoken language ; and it is a remarkable commentary on the poet's words that Mr. Wilmer, in 1859,[*] is found declaring that when he published an article on "Edgar A. Poe and his Calumniators," not a single paper noticed the vindicatory work, "whereas the whole press of the country seemed desirous of giving circulation and authenticity to the slanders." These facts—for *facts they are*—speak for themselves.

Noticeable reviews from the poet's pen in August were upon the Lives and Poetic Works of Margaret Davidson (one of Southey's *protégées*), and "L. E. L." The September number of *Graham's* contained the tale of "Never Bet the Devil your Head"—a skit at the "Moral"-mongers—and various book notices, the most interesting being a severe critique on Campbell for his

[*] *Vide " Our Press Gang ; or, a Complete Exposition of the Corruption and Crimes of the American Newspapers."*

"Life of Petrarch." Whilst deeming the Italian poet entitled to the highest consideration as a patriot, and for his zeal and judgment in the preservation of priceless literary treasures, Poe cannot refrain from confessing that he does not "regard the genius of Petrarch as a subject for enthusiastic admiration," nor the characteristics of his poetry as displaying traits of the highest, or even of a high, order. "Grace and tenderness" he grants him; "but these qualities are surely insufficient to establish his poetical apotheosis." A temporary absence from Philadelphia prevented Poe contributing to *Graham's* for October; but in November he commenced, and continued through three consecutive numbers, a series of papers on "Autography." These analyses of character were new, and different from the articles bearing a similar title published previously in the *Southern Literary Messenger;* they were more critical, more caustic, their author now more widely known, whilst the publication in which they appeared had a far larger and far more influential circulation, and, consequently, they created many more fresh enemies for their inditer.

## CHAPTER XIII.

### *REVERSES.*

THE closing month of 1841 left Edgar Poe in one of
the most brilliant and prosperous periods of his literary
career. The current volume of *Graham's Magazine*
ended in a blaze of triumph, the final page containing the statement that, "Perhaps the editors of no
magazine, either in America or Europe, ever sat
down at the close of a year to contemplate the progress of their work with more satisfaction than we do
now. Our success has been unexampled, almost incredible. We may assert, without fear of contradiction,
that no periodical ever witnessed the same increase
during so short a period. We began the year almost
unknown; certainly, far behind our contemporaries
in numbers; we close it with a list of twenty-five
thousand subscribers, and the insurance on every
hand that our popularity has as yet seen only its
dawning. But if such is the orient, what will our
noonday be?" Few can doubt but that this success—
unparalleled for those days—was due chiefly to the

talents of Edgar Poe. His tales, his essays, and, above
all, his undaunted critiques, inaugurated a series of
literary and pecuniary triumphs for the magazine and
its proprietor, although for the editor—the real creator
of this fortunate enterprise—little would seem to
have been gained beyond daily bread ; and misery
and misfortune, although temporarily repulsed, still
dogged his steps, ready to make him their prey once
more.

Poe's literary labours for 1842 began with the publication of "Eleanora," in the *Gift* for the current
year. This tale, so replete with personal revelations,
has already been adverted to in connection with the
poet's marriage. In *Graham's* for January appeared,
besides the last of the "Autography" articles, several
reviews, heralded by a vigorous *exordium* upon the condition of contemporary criticism in America. After
condemning anonymous reviewing, the prevalent gene-
ralising, and other vicious practices of the critics, Poe
argued with Bulwer that the reviewer " must have
courage to blame boldly, magnanimity to eschew envy,
genius to appreciate, learning to compare, an eye for
beauty, an ear for music, and a heart for feeling," to
all of which requirements Poe added, " a talent for
analysis, and a solemn indifference to abuse." In a
notice of the "Vicar of Wakefield," described as
" one of the most admirable fictions in the language,"

some admirable remarks upon the subject of illustrating books are made, and various characteristic utterances —utterances as yet not reproduced—are given, upon Heber, Walpole, "Christopher North," and other more or less known writers. The February number of the magazine contained an article on Brainard, one of the pioneers of American literature, and a fresh and eulogistic review of "Barnaby Rudge," whilst the number for March included, amongst minor notices, analyses of new books by or about Lever, Longfellow, Howitt, and Brougham. In *Graham's* for April appeared the tale of "Life in Death," or "The Oval Portrait," as it was subsequently renamed. The thesis of this story is somewhat similar to one of Hawthorne's "Twice-Told Tales," and although containing a few Poësque touches, such as the hero's embarrassment as to the quantity of opium to be eaten, it does not call for extended comment. A far more important contribution to this number was a lengthy review of Longfellow's "Ballads," in the course of which Poe took occasion to propound his fixed idea that BEAUTY, and Beauty *only*, should be the theme of Art. If Truth were the chief object, the highest aim of Art, then, as he truly declares, "Jan Steen was a greater artist than Angelo, and Crabbe is a nobler poet than Milton." In uttering an earnest protest against those who deem the work should be subservient to its moral, he re-

proaches his brother poet for the confirmed didacticism
of his tone; " that this mode of procedure will find
stern defenders," he says, " should never excite surprise, so long as the world is full to overflowing with
cant and conventicles. There are men who will
scramble on all fours through the muddiest sloughs of
vice to pick up a single apple of virtue." What may
be termed the articles of his artistic creed are simply
and severely summed up in these remarks, which will
call forth a sympathetic echo in the hearts of all true
worshippers of the Beautiful:—

"Now, with as deep a reverence for 'the true' as ever
inspired the bosom of mortal man, we would limit, in many
respects, its modes of inculcation. We would limit to enforce them. We would not render them impotent by dissipation. The demands of truth are severe. She has no
sympathy with the myrtles. All that is indispensable in
song is all with which she has nothing to do. To deck her
in gay robes is to render her a harlot. It is but making her
a flaunting paradox to wreathe her in gems and flowers.
Even in stating this our present proposition, we verify our
own words—we feel the necessity, in enforcing this *truth,*
of descending from metaphor. Let us then be simple and
distinct. To convey 'the true' we are required to dismiss
from the attention all inessentials. We must be perspicuous,
precise, terse. We need concentration rather than expansion
of mind. We must be calm, unimpassioned, unexcited—
in a word, we must be in that peculiar mood which, as
nearly as possible, is the exact converse of the poetical.
He must be blind indeed who cannot perceive the radical

and chasmal difference between the truthful and the poetical modes of inculcation. He must be grossly wedded to conventionalisms who, in spite of this difference, shall still attempt to reconcile the obstinate oils and waters of Poetry and Truth. . . .

"We would define in brief the Poetry of words as the *Rhythmical Creation of Beauty*. Beyond the limits of Beauty its province does not extend. Its sole arbiter is Taste. With the Intellect or with the Conscience it has only collateral relations. It has no dependence, unless incidentally, upon either Duty or *Truth*. That our definition will necessarily exclude much of what, through a supine toleration, has been hitherto ranked as poetical, is a matter which affords us not even momentary concern. We address but the thoughtful, and heed only their approval—with our own. If our suggestions are truthful, then 'after many days' shall they be understood as truth, even though found in contradiction of *all* that has been hitherto so understood. If false, shall we not be the first to bid them die?"

In summing up his observations upon the aims of true Art, Poe deems that, of the poets who have appeared most fully instinct with the principles he enunciates, Keats should be mentioned as the most remarkable; "he is," he declares, "the sole British poet who has never erred in his themes. Beauty is always his aim."

Much as the present, or the forthcoming generation may be inclined to accept these *dicta* as the veritable gospel of Poesy, they are scarcely likely to have gained Poe much κυδος from the half-educated critics, moral-mongers, and petty poetasters, amid whom he had to earn his daily bread; and their triumph was at hand. With this April number of *Graham's*, his editorial connection with the magazine ceased, although the following issue contained several book notices from his pen, as well as a characteristic tale, "The Masque of the Red Death"—well named "a Fantasy" by its author. A review of Hawthorne, commenced in this and completed in the next number, contains some noteworthy passages, especially if they be read in the knowledge that they were published when their subject was almost unknown, and yet was then designated by Poe as the highest and most meritorious prose writer of America. He says:—

"The style of Mr. Hawthorne is purity itself. His *tone* is singularly effective—wild, plaintive, thoughtful, and in full accordance with his themes. We have only to object that there is insufficient diversity in these themes themselves, or rather in their character. His *originality* both of incident and of reflection is very remarkable; and this trait alone would ensure him at least *our* warmest regard and commendation. . . . We look upon him as one of the few men of indisputable genius to whom our country has as yet given birth."

And again, with complete self-abnegation and absence of all jealousy :—" Of Mr. Hawthorne's Tales we would say, emphatically, that they belong to the highest region of Art—an Art subservient to genius of a very lofty order. We know of few compositions which the critic can more honestly commend than these ' Twice-Told Tales.' As Americans, we feel proud of the book." Another paragraph, in praise of these productions, doubtless, excited a flutter of indignant expostulation from the thousand and one forgotten notorieties who beheld themselves so scornfully overlooked by the critic:—" We have very few American tales of real merit; we may say, indeed, none, with the exception of ' The Tales of a Traveller ' of Washington Irving, and these ' Twice-Told Tales ' of Mr. Hawthorne. Some of the pieces of Mr. John Neal abound in vigor and originality; but, in general, his compositions of this class are excessively diffuse, extravagant, and indicative of an imperfect sentiment of Art."

For months the poet's story has been little more than a record of his literary labour, but once again his personal history—" unmerciful disaster "—intervenes, and henceforth his career is one of anguish and terror. With the April number, as above stated, Poe's editorial management of *Graham's Magazine* ceased. During the eighteen months that he had directed the destinies of the publication, its circulation had increased from five to fifty-two thousand, and its reputation had spread even across the Atlantic, English and French *literati* both contributing to and drawing allusions from its pages. This being so, and the poet's *régime* productive of such brilliant results, why was the connection severed ? Mr. Graham, the magazine's proprietor, says of Poe—and his words prove no quarrel terminated the editorship :—" He had the docility and kind-heartedness of a child. No man was more quickly touched by a kindness, none more prompt to atone for an injury. For three or four years I knew him intimately, and for eighteen months saw him almost daily ; much of the time writing or conversing at the same desk ; knowing all his hopes, his fears, and little annoyances of life, as well as his high-hearted struggle with adverse fate— yet he was always the same polished gentleman—the quiet, unobtrusive, thoughtful scholar — the devoted husband—frugal in his personal expenses—punctual and unwearied in his industry — and the *soul of honour* in all his transactions. This, of course, was in his better days, and by them *we* judge the man. But even after his habits had changed, there was no literary man to whom I would more readily advance money for labour to be done."

Probably the whole truth as to Poe's resignation of this editorship will never be known ; doubtless, it was due to a combination of causes. There was the constitutional restlessness—the " nervous restlessness —which," as he acknowledges, " haunted me as a

fiend," and which at times overpowered him, and
drove him from place to place in a vain search for the
El Dorado of his hopes; there was the ever-lingering
desire to found a magazine of his own, and, what must
be confessed, the beginning of those "irregularities"
which, during the remainder of his life, at certain
more or less lengthy intervals, destroyed his hopes and
placed his reputation in the power of implacable foes.
The origin of this fearsome scourge—which was not the
outcome of youthful excesses, as maliciously asserted
—is to be traced to the most terrible episode in
the unfortunate poet's career.   In a letter to an old
and esteemed correspondent, dated January 4, 1848,
Poe thus unbosoms himself of his secret—a secret as
gruesome as any told of in the most terrible of his
tales :—

"You say, 'Can you *hint* to me what was the 'terrible
evil' which caused the 'irregularities' so profoundly la-
mented ?'*   Yes, I can do more than hint.   This 'evil' was
the greatest which can befall a man.   Six years ago,
a wife, whom I loved as no man ever loved before, ruptured
a blood-vessel in singing.   Her life was despaired of.   I took
leave of her forever, and underwent all the agonies of her
death.   She recovered partially, and I again hoped.   At the
end of a year, the vessel broke again.   I went through precisely the same scene. . . . Then again—again—and even
once again, at varying intervals.   Each time I felt all the

---

* *Vide* the Reply to Thomas Dunn English, p 81, vol. ii.

agonies of her death—and at each accession of the disorder I
loved her more dearly and clung to her life with more desperate pertinacity. But I am constitutionally sensitive—nervous
in a very unusual degree. I became insane, with long
intervals of horrible sanity. During these fits of absolute
unconsciousness, I drank—God only knows how often or how
much. As a matter of course, my enemies referred the insanity to the drink, rather than the drink to the insanity.
I had, indeed, nearly abandoned all hope of a permanent
cure, when I found one in the *death* of my wife. This I can
and do endure as becomes a man. It was the horrible never-
ending oscillation between hope and despair which I could
*not* longer have endured, without total loss of reason. In
the death of what was my life, then, I receive a new, but—
Oh God !—how melancholy an existence."

Although the unveiling this terrible mystery in the
poet's life almost resembles sacrilege, it is better that
the truth be bared, than that the false impressions—
purposely or unintentionally created—should continue
as to Poe's accredited habits of dissipation. No one
who really knew the man, either personally or through
his works, but will believe him when he asserted, " I
have absolutely *no* pleasure in the stimulants in which
I sometimes so madly indulge. It has not been in
the pursuit of pleasure that I have perilled life and
reputation and reason. It has been in the desperate
attempt to escape from torturing memories." * Doubtless, there are weighty reasons why this moral cancer,

* Letter to Mrs. S. H. Whitman.

which ate so deeply into the poet's health and happiness, should have remained unrevealed; but, in this history of his life concealment is as impossible as it is, apparently, needless,—he only has been the sufferer, personally and posthumously.

Previous, however, to Poe's resignation of the *Graham Magazine* editorship, the unhappy catastrophe had already happened to his idolised wife, and the hoping against hope, and relapses into fits of maddening despair, had already begun to exert their deleterious effects upon him, causing a gradual but slow deterioration of his whole moral, physical, and intellectual nature. Mr. Graham, in his eloquent defence of the poet against the defamation of Griswold,[*] thus alludes to domestic ties and troubles :—

"I shall never forget how solicitous of the happiness of his wife and mother-in law he was, whilst one of the editors of *Graham's Magazine ;* his whole efforts seemed to be to procure the comfort and welfare of his home. Except for their happiness, and the natural ambition of having a magazine of his own, I never heard him deplore the want of wealth. The truth is, he cared little for money, and knew less of its value, for he seemed to have no personal

---

[*] R. W. Griswold was an employé of Mr. Graham, and, it is alleged, was dismissed for dishonesty. Thackeray, when in America, detected him in deliberate lying, and it was through his falsehoods that Messrs. Harper & Brothers had to pay Charles Dickens a larger sum than anticipated for "advance sheets" of "Bleak House."—J. H. I.

expenses. What he received from me in regular monthly instalments went directly into the hands of his mother-in-law for family comforts ; and *twice* only I remember his purchasing some rather expensive luxuries for his house, and then he was nervous to the degree of misery until he had, by extra articles, covered what he considered an imprudent indebtedness. His love for his wife was a sort of rapturous worship of the spirit of beauty, which he felt was fading before his eyes. I have seen him hovering around her when she was ill, with all the fond fear and tender anxiety of a mother for her first-born—her slightest cough causing in him a shudder, a heart chill, that was visible. I rode out one summer evening with them, and the remembrance of his watchful eyes, eagerly bent upon the slightest change of hue in that loved face, haunts me yet as the memory of a sad strain. It was this hourly *anticipation* of her loss, that made him a sad and thoughtful man, and lent a mournful melody to his undying song." *

This adoration of and fidelity to his youthful wife is a trait in Poe's character that no one *personally* acquainted with the hapless pair ever denied, even the poet's most inveterate enemies acknowledged the fact. But when he was dead, and helpless to repudiate the slander, persons who assume to have had his confidence, and to have been his friends, yet knew him only in the last moments of his life, declare that the union with Virginia Clemm was only a marriage of convenience, and that Poe never had any real affection for her. Mrs. Osgood, who, undoubtedly, knew more

* *Graham's Magazine,* March 1850.

of the poet's innermost feelings during the last five
years of his life than any person outside his domestic
circle, said of his wife, " I believe she was the only
woman whom he ever truly loved; and this is
evidenced by the exquisite pathos of the little poem
lately written, called ' Annabel Lee,' of which she was
the subject, and which is by far the most natural,
simple, tender, and touchingly beautiful of all his
songs. I have heard it said that it was intended to
illustrate a late love affair of the author; but they
who believe this have, in their dulness, evidently misunderstood or missed the beautiful meaning latent in
the most lovely of all its verses, where he says,—

> ' A wind blew out of a cloud, chilling
> My beautiful Annabel Lee,
> So that her *highborn kinsmen* came,
> And bore her away from me.'

There seems a strange and almost profane disregard
of the sacred purity and spiritual tenderness of this
delicious ballad, in thus overlooking the allusion to
the *kindred angels* and the heavenly *Father* of the lost
and loved and unforgotten wife."

The long-tried affection displayed for each other by
the poet and Mrs. Clemm was, undoubtedly, the result
of the mutual love they bore, and knew each other
bore, for the departed Virginia. In the well-known

sonnet addressed to his mother-in-law—his "more than mother"—Poe says, in language we hold no evidence to question the truth and earnestness of,—

> " My mother—my own mother, who died early,
>     Was but the mother of myself; but you
> Are mother to the one I loved so dearly,
>     And thus are dearer than the mother I knew
> By that infinity with which my wife
> Was dearer to my soul than its soul-life."

Mrs. Clemm clung to the poet, and watched and waited upon him after her daughter's death, because *she knew* how devoted a husband he had been. "It is utterly false," she asserted at the first promulgation of this slander—lately revived, for easily apparent purposes —" It is utterly false the report of his being faithless or unkind to her (Virginia). He was devoted to her until the last hour of her death, as all our friends can testify. . . . I enclose you two of Eddie's letters. . . . The other was written at the time you generously offered to take my darling Virginia. I wrote to Eddie asking his advice, and this is his answer. Does the affection then expressed look as if he could ever cease to love her ? And he never did."*

A writer in a New York journal, and, apparently, a personal acquaintance of Poe, says, " It was one of the saddest things in his sad history that the two

---

* Letter from Maria Clemm to Neilson Poe, August 26, 1860.

dearest to him were sharers of his hardships and sufferings—his beautiful young wife and her devoted mother. He married his cousin, who was brought up at the South, and was as unused to toil as she was unfit for it. She hardly looked more than fourteen, fair, soft, and graceful and girlish. Every one who saw her was won by her. Poe was very proud and very fond of her, and used to delight in the round, childlike face and plump little finger, which he contrasted with himself, so thin and half-melancholy looking, and she in turn idolised him. She had a voice of wonderful sweetness, and was an exquisite singer, and in some of their more prosperous days, when they were living in a pretty little rose-covered cottage on the outskirts of Philadelphia, she had her harp and piano."*

At the time to which this writer refers the Poes appear to have resided in Coates Street, Fairmount, whence they removed to North Seven Street, Spring Garden, in the suburbs of the city. Some pleasant reminiscences of the poet and his family, as the household was in this pretty Pennsylvanian home, have been furnished to us by Captain Mayne Reid and others. After describing the charming little suburban dwelling, with its floral bedecked porch, and its tasteful although inexpensive furniture, Captain Reid proceeds to de-

* A. B. Harris, in *Hearth and Home*, 1870.

scribe its inmates, as he knew them, personally as well
as by repute. " Poe," he says, " I have known for a
whole month closeted in his house, all the time hard
at work with his pen, poorly paid, and hard driven to
keep the wolf from his slightly-fastened door; intruded on only by a few select friends, who always
found him, what they knew him to be, a generous
host, an affectionate son-in-law and husband,—in
short, a respectable gentleman. . . . In the list of
literary men there has been no such spiteful biographer
as Rufus Griswold, and never such a victim of posthumous spite as poor Edgar Allan Poe." *

The poet's wife is referred to by the Captain as,
" A lady angelically beautiful in person, and not less
beautiful in spirit. No one who remembers that dark-
eyed, dark-haired daughter of Virginia,†—her own
name—her grace, her facial beauty, her demeanour,
so modest as to be remarkable ; no one who has ever
spent an hour in her company, but will endorse what
I have said. I remember how we, the friends of the
poet, used to talk of her high qualities, and when we
talked of her beauty, I well knew that the rose-tint
upon her cheek was too bright, too pure to be of earth.
It was consumption's colour, that sadly beautiful light
that beckons to an early tomb."

* " A Dead Man Defended," in *Onward* for April 1869.
† Virginia Poe was a native of Maryland.—J. H. I.

Mrs. Clemm, the poet's aunt, the mother of his wife, was still the presiding spirit of their little domicile, and of her the Englishman says, " Besides the poet and his interesting wife, there was but one other dweller. It was a woman of middle age and almost masculine aspect. She had the size and figure of a man, with a countenance that, at first sight, seemed scarce feminine. A stranger would have been incredulous, surprised, as I was, when introduced to her as the mother of that angelic creature who had accepted Edgar Poe as the partner of her life. She was the ever vigilant guardian of the house, watching it against the ever silent but continuous sap of necessity, that appeared every day to be approaching closer and nearer. She was the sole servant, keeping everything clean ; the sole messenger, doing the errands, making pilgrimages between the poet and his publishers, frequently bringing back such chilling responses as, ' The article not accepted,' or, ' The cheque not to be given until such and such a day '—often too late for his necessities."

Mr. A. B. Harris, the author already quoted from, proceeds to relate of the residence in Spring Garden, that " It was during their stay there that Mrs. Poe, while singing one evening, ruptured a blood-vessel, and after that she suffered a hundred deaths. She could not bear the slightest exposure, and needed the utmost care ; and all those conveniences as to apartment and surroundings which are so important in the case of an invalid were almost matters of life and death to her. And yet the room where she lay for weeks, hardly able to breathe, except as she was fanned, was a little place with the ceiling so low over the narrow bed that her head almost touched it. But no one dared to speak, Mr. Poe was so sensitive and irritable; 'quick as steel and flint,' said one who knew him in those days. And he would not allow a word about the danger of her dying, the mention of it drove him wild."

Not only did the mention of the danger of his wife's death drive Poe wild, but the thoughts of it evidently rendered him unfit for literary work. Unable to provide the comforts needed for her dearest to him, to have to see his anxieties and privations shared by her, drove the poet to the brink of madness. Powerless to provide for the necessities at home, " he would steal out of the house at night," says Mr. Harris, " and go off and wander about the streets for hours, proud, heartsick, despairing, not knowing which way to turn, or what to do, while Mrs. Clemm would endure the anxiety at home as long as she could and then start off in search of him.

" So they lived, bound together in tender bonds of love and sorrow—their love making their lot more tolerable—the three clinging to each other; and the

mother was the good angel who strove to shield the
poet and save him. This way their lives went on in
those dark days; he trying desperately at times to
earn money, writing a little, and fitfully fighting
against himself, sustained only by their solace and
sympathy, and by the helping hand of the self-sacrificing mother, who loved him as if he had been, indeed,
her own son."

Unable to secure a certain income by literature—
for it must be remembered that even in his best days
his receipts were but small, and, at best, chiefly
dependent upon the caprice or continuous goodwill of
an employer—the unfortunate poet appears to have
thought the attainment of a government post would at
least secure him from utter dependence. His literary
correspondent, Mr. F. W. Thomas, had recently obtained
a situation under government, and Poe hoped, through
the influence of his various friends and acquaintances,
to be able to do the same; at any rate he determined
to try, and the following letter to John Neal would
appear to refer to this attempt :—

"PHILADELPHIA, *June* 4.

"MY DEAR SIR,—As you gave me the first jog in my literary
career, you are in a manner bound to protect me and keep
me rolling. I therefore now ask you to aid me with your
influence in whatever manner your experience shall suggest.
It strikes me that I never write to you except to ask a favour,

but my friend Thomas will assure you that I bear you always in mind, holding you in the highest respect and esteem.—Most truly yours,                    EDGAR A. POE.

"JOHN NEAL, Esq."

Several of the poet's influential friends were, doubtless, appealed to, and the following extracts have been given by an American journalist as portions of two letters written on the 26th of June and 4th of July respectively to the late F. W. Thomas : *—

"Would to God I could do as you have done! Do you seriously think that an application to Tyler would have a good result? My claims, to be sure, are few. I am a Virginian, at least I call myself one, for I have resided all my life, until within the last few years, in Richmond. My political principles have always been, as nearly as may be, with the existing administration, and I battled with right good will for Harrison when opportunity offered. With Mr. Tyler I have some slight personal acquaintance—although this is a matter which he has possibly forgotten. For the rest, I am a literary man, and I see a disposition in Government to cherish letters. Have I any chance?"

Mr. Thomas probably held forth some kind of hope to the distracted poet, as this second communication followed fast upon the above :—

"I wish to God I could visit Washington—but the old story, you know—I have no money—not even enough to

---

* "Memoir of Edgar Allan Poe," by R. H. Stoddard, pp. 66–69.

take me there, saying nothing of getting back. It is a hard thing to be poor—but as I am kept so by an honest motive, I dare not complain. Your suggestion about Mr. Kennedy is well timed; and here, Thomas, you can do me a true service. Call upon Kennedy—you know him I believe—if not, introduce yourself, he is a perfect gentleman, and will give you a cordial welcome. Speak to him of my wishes, and urge him to see the Secretary of War in my behalf—or one of the other Secretaries, or President Tyler. I mention in particular the Secretary of War, because I have been to W. Point, and this may stand me in some stead. I would be glad to get almost any appointment—even a $500 one—so that I may have something independent of letters for a subsistence. To coin one's brain into silver, at the nod of a master, is to my thinking the hardest task in the world. Mr. Kennedy has been at all times a true friend to me—he was the first true friend I ever had—I am indebted to him *for life itself.* He will be willing to help me, I know—but *needs urging,* for he is always head and ears in business. Thomas, may I depend upon you ? "

Whether Mr. Thomas found time and inclination to prosecute his friend's desires or not, is, of course, unknown, but that the unfortunate poet did not obtain an appointment is but too well known. Could he have procured a permanent government post, it would have lifted him above the most galling petty pecuniary anxieties of the hour, and have left him some leisure, some power, to produce more of his highly-polished and more artistic labours, instead of leaving him to fritter away his genius in hasty and crude work. After

Poe's severance from *Graham's*, his wife's illness, and, during its height, his own inability to write, are declared to have reduced the little household almost to starvation. "There was then," says Mr. Harris, "some kind of a society under the care of ladies for helping in a delicate way those who were in need, and would signify it by depositing some articles at the rooms—persons whom common charity could not reach; and to that Mrs. Clemm, the mother, made application. Yet so sensitive and proud was the little family, that it was almost impossible to aid them to any extent, even when they were suffering for the common comforts of life." Of course these terrible struggles with illness and poverty were not continuous ; occasional bursts of hope broke through the clouds of "unmerciful disaster," and whenever the prospects brightened, the poet plied his pen with renewed vigour. In October, Mr. Graham's magazine published a critique by Poe on " Rufus Dawes," one of the forgotten two hundred celebrities of Mr. Griswold's pantheon. Of him —the then famous now forgotten " poet "—Poe said, "We hesitate not to say that no man in America has been more shamefully over-estimated." "We say shamefully," he adds, " for . . . the laudation in this instance, as it stands upon record, must be regarded as a laughable although bitter satire upon the general zeal, accuracy, and independence of that critical spirit

which, but a few years ago, pervaded and degraded
the land." After a stringent review of the works of
Mr. Dawes, the poet proceeds to remark that that
gentleman is known for his amiability and for his
many friends, which may have enhanced his literary
reputation.  " We shall not here insist upon the fact
that *we*," says Poe, " bear him no personal ill-will.
With those who know us, such a declaration would
appear supererogatory ; and by those who know us
not it would, doubtless, be received with incredulity.
What we have said, however, is *not* in opposition to
Mr. Dawes, nor even so much in opposition to the
poems of Mr. Dawes, as in defence of the many true
souls which, in Mr. Dawes's apotheosis, are aggrieved.
The laudation of the unworthy is to the worthy the
most bitter of all wrong.  But it is unbecoming in
him who merely demonstrates a truth to offer reason
or apology for the demonstration."

These critiques were, of course, continually enlargen-
ing the circle of the poet's foes and shutting him out
from publications where, had he been contented to, or,
perhaps, permitted by publishers to, have written
only tales and poems, his services would have been
eagerly sought for.  After having been long promised
to the reading public as about to write for Snowden's
*Lady's Companion*, that journal at last, in October
1842, published "The Landscape Garden," subse-

quently enlarged and called " The Domain of Arnheim,"
from his admired but dreaded pen. This essay, for
it can scarcely be styled a tale, is used as a medium
by the poet for the expression of his views on the
employment of personal wealth in the pursuit of happiness. As the peg whereon to hang several of his own
views of society he selects the common idea—" a
grossly exaggerated one," as he admits—as to the
amount of property accumulated in the celebrated
Thelluson case, and proceeds to depict the ideas and
aims of the presumed inheritor of this immense fortune,
this fabled " ninety millions of pounds." In the contemplation of this enormous wealth the mind of Edgar
Poe could find at once scope for his imagination and
solace for his cravings after splendour. The opinions
and idiosyncrasies of the hero of the sketch are the
barely hidden opinions and idiosyncrasies of the poet
himself, and as such are doubly interesting to his readers.
A believer in the reality of happiness, although never
the possessor of that chimera, he thus discourses on the
theme :—" In the brief existence of Ellison I fancy that
I have seen refuted the dogma, that in man's very
nature lies some hidden principle, the antagonist of
bliss. An anxious examination of his career has given
me to understand that, in general, from the violation
of a few simple laws of humanity arises the wretched-
ness of mankind ; that as a species we have in our

possession the as yet unwrought elements of content ; and that, even now, in the present darkness and madness of all thought on the great question of the social condition, it is not impossible that man, the individual, under certain unusual and highly fortuitous conditions, may be happy."

To refute this proposition—the premises providing for the indefinite " unusual and highly fortuitous conditions "—may be difficult ; but a palpable fallacy appears to lurk in the poet's further suggestion that " while a high order of genius is necessarily ambitious, the highest is above that which is termed ambition. And may it not thus happen," he demands, " that many far greater than Milton have contentedly remained mute and inglorious ? " " I believe," is his avowed conclusion, " that the world has never seen—and that, unless through some series of accidents goading the noblest order of mind into distasteful exertion, the world will never see—that full extent of triumphant execution in the richer domains of art, of which the human nature is absolutely capable." Of course, as in the previous case, the poet has allowed himself a certain loophole of escape, in the apparent fact that the greatest genius being contented to remain unknown, the existence of his superior capability cannot be disproved, but to us it appears self-evident that genius is itself the motive power that impels to production, and the greater the genius the stronger the impulse to produce, irrespective of " distasteful exertion " or impediment.

The elements of happiness, as propounded by the creator of Arnheim's gorgeous domain, apply more strictly to the seeker after physical rather than mental enjoyment, and his third elementary principle might seem to be contradictory to the fourth ; these are his conditions of earthly bliss :—" That which he considered chief was the simple and purely physical one of free exercise in the open air. . . . His second condition was the love of woman. His third, and most difficult of realisation, was the contempt of ambition. His fourth was an object of unceasing pursuit." That Ellison, or, rather, his *alter ego*, Poe, should have little or no faith in the possibility of the improvement of the general condition of man, is scarcely surprising, although it hardly accords with the doctrines he is presupposed to have imbibed from Condorcet and other Human Perfectibility advocates. In his proposition that the elements of beauty in art are as certain and as unchangeable, although not so demonstrable, as the rules of mathematics, he will have the credence and sympathy of all his brethren. His suggestion that genius cannot be gained by study of rules, although rules may be adduced from works of genius —that " we may be instructed to build a ' Cato ' (*i.e.*,

Addison's), but we are in vain told *how* to conceive a
Parthenon or an ' Inferno' "—is, indeed, little more
than a new application of the old adage *poeta nascitur
non fit*. But "The Domain of Arnheim," apart from any
interest it may derive from its author's personal views,
will always charm the intelligent reader by its gorgeous
and glowing scenery—the comprehensive realisation
of a poet's vast and most exuberant imagination.

In November Snowden's *Lady's Companion* began
the publication of "The Mystery of Marie Roget," one
of the most marvellous examples of Poe's capability
of dealing with, and analysing, the mysteries of the
human mind. This tale, which occupied a large portion of three monthly numbers of the journal in which
it was first issued, made a profound impression upon
the public, not that it was so interesting as a work of
art as many of its predecessors from the same pen, but
from the fact that it referred to real and widely-known
circumstances. To some extent the story is a sequel,
or rather sequence, of "The Murders in the Rue
Morgue," and purports to be carried on, so far as the
mere spectators of the tragedy are concerned, by the
same personages ; but whilst that was pure fiction
from beginning to end, this recital refers to fact, that
is to say, to · fact but slightly veiled. The author
furnishes the following preliminary words in explanation of the general design of his narrative :—

"A young girl, Mary Cecilia Rogers, was murdered in the vicinity of New York; and although her death occasioned an intense and long-enduring excitement, the mystery attending it had remained unsolved at the period when the present paper was written and published. Herein, under pretence of relating the fate of a Parisian *grisette*, the author has followed in minute detail the essential, while merely paralleling the inessential, facts of the real murder of Mary Rogers. Thus all argument founded upon the fiction is applicable to the truth; and the investigation of truth was the object. 'The Mystery of Marie Roget' was composed at a distance from the scene of the atrocity, and with no other means of investigation than the newspapers afforded. Thus much escaped the writer of which he could have availed himself, had he been on the spot, and visited the localities. It may not be improper to record, nevertheless, that the confessions of *two* persons (one of them the 'Madame Deluc' of the narrative), made at different periods, long subsequent to the publication, confirmed in full, not only the general conclusion, but absolutely *all* the chief hypothetical details by which that conclusion was attained."

Poe, under the garb of the magazine's editor, concludes the narrative thus: "For reasons which we shall not specify, but which to many readers will appear obvious, we have taken the liberty of here omitting, from the MSS. placed in our hands [by Mr. Poe], such portion as details the *following up* of the apparently slight clue obtained !" Latterly it has been the fashion (especially by foreigners) to disbelieve that Marie Roget's mystery had any real existence, and that the whole recital was the coinage of the poet's brain, and the notes only appended to give it an air of *vraisemblance.* Nevertheless, such was not the case ; the narrative *was* founded on fact, although the incidents of the tragedy differed widely from those recounted in the tale. The naval officer implicated was named Spencer. In a letter to a literary friend asking about the omitted portions of the manuscript, above referred to, Poe says, " Nothing was omitted in 'Marie Roget' but what I omitted myself—all *that* is mystification. . . . The 'naval officer,' who committed the murder (rather the accidental death arising from an attempt at abortion) *confessed* it ; and the whole matter is now well understood ; but, for the sake of relatives, I must not speak further."

This narrative, or rather this analysis of the Unknown by ratiocination, is, presumedly, based upon the fact that even *chance* may be made a matter of absolute calculation. The subject was peculiarly suited to the mind of Poe, a mind in which mathematical accuracy was balanced by lofty imagination tinged by superstition. "There are few persons," he remarks, "even among the calmest thinkers, who have not occasionally been startled into a vague yet thrilling half-credence in the supernatural *by coincidences* of so seemingly marvellous a character that, as *mere* coincidences, the intellect has been unable to receive them. Such sentiments—for the half-credences of which I speak have never the full force of *thought*—such sentiments are seldom thoroughly stifled unless by reference to the doctrine of chance, or, as it is technically termed, the Calculus of Probabilities. Now this calculus is in its essence purely mathematical; and thus we have the anomaly of the most rigidly exact in science applied to the shadow and spirituality of the most intangible in speculation."

Recurring to this doctrine, he continues :—

"Experience has shown, and a true philosophy will always show, that a vast, perhaps the larger portion of truth, arises from the seemingly irrelevant. It is through the spirit of this principle, if not precisely through its letter, that modern science has resolved to *calculate upon the unforeseen*. But perhaps you do not comprehend me. The history of human knowledge has so uninterruptedly shown that to collateral, or incidental, or accidental events, we are indebted for the most numerous and most valuable discoveries, that it has at length become necessary, in any prospective view of improvement, to make not only large, but the largest allowances for inventions that shall arise by chance, and quite out of the range of ordinary expectation. It is no longer philosophical to base upon what has been a vision of what is to be. *Accident* is admitted as a portion of the substructure. We make chance a matter of absolute calculation. We subject the unlooked for and unimagined to the mathematical *formulæ* of the schools. I repeat that it is no more than fact that the *larger* portion of all truth has sprung from the collateral."

Analogous speculations form the bases of other succeeding stories, such as "The Purloined Letter" and "The Gold Bug," hereafter to be referred to. There is, however, another reference in "The Mystery of Marie Roget" to an all-important and but-too-rarely-alluded-to truth, the vital importance of which cannot be over-estimated—the effects of which, however, are beheld and experienced much more injuriously in America than in the Old World :—

"We should bear in mind," is the commentary, "that in general it is the object of our newspapers rather to create a sensation—to make a point—than to further the cause of truth. The latter end is only pursued when it seems coincident with the former. The print which merely falls in with ordinary opinion (however well founded this opinion may be), earns for itself no credit with the mob. The mass of the people regard as profound only him who suggests *pungent contradictions* of the general idea. In ratiocination, not less than in literature, it is the *epigram* which is the most immediately and the most universally appreciated. In both, it is of the lowest order of merit."

*The Gift* for 1843 contained "The Pit and the

Pendulum," a tale of less philosophical value, perhaps,
than the class of works just alluded to, but of intense
fascination to the general reader.   It is founded upon,
or rather suggested by, the terrible sufferings of a
Spanish refugee, who closed his miserable career amid
the company of actors to which Poe's mother belonged,
and it would be interesting to discover how the story
reached the poet's knowledge.   The author of this tale
of the Inquisition's tortures, reproduces in its earliest
sentences somewhat similar psychological fancies to
those found in the " Colloquy of Monos and Una," but
richer in tone and riper in experience.   There is a
truth and suggestiveness in the following passages which
can be recognised and appreciated by many who would
fail to grasp the shadowy hints of the earlier work :—

" Even in the grave all *is not* lost.   Else there is no
immortality for man.   Arousing from the most profound of
slumbers, we break the gossamer web of *some* dream.   Yet
in a second afterwards (so frail may that web have been) we
remember not that we have dreamed.   In the return to life
from the swoon there are two stages : first, that of the sense
of mental or spiritual ; secondly, that of the sense of physical
existence.   It seems probable that if, upon reaching the
second stage, we could recall the impressions of the first, we
should find these impressions eloquent in memories of the
gulf beyond.   And that gulf is—what ?   How at least shall
we distinguish its shadows from those of the tomb ?   But if
the impressions of what I have termed the first stage are not
at will recalled, yet, after long interval, do they not come

unbidden, while we marvel whence they come? He who
has never swooned is not he who finds strange palaces and
wildly familiar faces in coals that glow; is not he who beholds
floating in mid-air the sad visions that the many may not
view; is not he who ponders over the perfume of some novel
flower; is not he whose brain grows bewildered with the
meaning of some musical cadence which has never before
arrested his attention.

"Amid frequent and thoughtful endeavours to remember,
amid earnest struggles to regather some token of the state
of seeming nothingness into which my soul had lapsed, there
have been moments when I have dreamed of success; there
have been brief, very brief periods when I have con-
jured up remembrances which the lucid reason of a later
epoch assures me could have had reference only to that
condition of seeming unconsciousness."

Another noteworthy point about this story is the
artistic accuracy of taste displayed in what may be
regarded by some as mere minor details; for instance,
instead of a description of the concrete horrors, such
as a commonplace mind would have given, of the in-
terior of the *pit*, the imagination only is appealed to
and all its terror is *suggested* but left untold. What
a far finer instinct, and more profound knowledge of
art, does this restraint imply, than if the narrator had
afforded a circumstantial account of some such loath-
some mediæval pit as is the one, for instance, shown at
Baden-Baden. The idea of the collapsing chamber,
also, unlike in other tales in which that oft-told-of

apparatus of torture plays a part, is made subservient to the other purposes of the work, rather than they to it.

Upon leaving Mr. Graham, Poe once more exerted himself towards carrying into execution his life-long scheme of a magazine of his own.  He wrote to his friends in various parts of the States, issued prospectuses from time to time, and for a long while did his best, but in vain, to resuscitate his embryo periodical.  Ultimately he induced Mr. Thomas C. Clarke, a Philadelphia publisher, and founder and editor of several well-known publications, to join him in his speculation.  Poe, as literary and art critic for the *Saturday Evening Post*—for many years one of the most popular and flourishing journals of its kind in the country—had already afforded Mr. Clarke, who was the proprietor, evidence of his literary and editoral ability. Accordingly, on January 31, 1843, Mr. Clarke took Edgar Poe into partnership, so far, at least, as the projected periodical was concerned, and issued a prospectus and other publications connected with it signed " Clarke and Poe."  The address to the journals and anticipated contributors, alluding to the prospectus which had already been circulated of the proposed *Penn Magazine,* stated that that project had been suspended through circumstances of no interest to the public, and that it had now been resumed, under the best auspices, subject only to a change of title.    The name given to the stillborn journal had been deemed too local in its suggestions, it was, therefore, proposed to adopt that of *The Stylus* for the new speculation. Allusion was made to "the general knowledge, on the part of the public," of Poe's former connection with the *Southern Literary Messenger*, and *Graham's Magazine*, and such knowledge, it was pre-supposed, obviated the necessity for any very rigid definition of the literary character or aims of the new publication. "In many important points, however," said Poe, "the new magazine will differ widely from either of those named. It will endeavour to be more varied, more vigorous, more pungent, more original, more individual, and more independent." Again, referring to the two periodicals with which his connections had been best known, he said:—

"I shall be pardoned for speaking more directly of the two magazines in question. Having in neither of them any proprietary right, the objects of their very worthy owners, too, being in many respects at variance with my own, I found it not only impossible to effect anything on the score of taste for their mechanical or external appearance, but difficult to stamp upon them internally that *individuality* which I believed essential to their success. In regard to the extensive and permanent influence of such publications, it appears to me that continuity, distinctness, and a marked certainty of purpose, are requisites of vital importance; but attainable only when one mind alone has at least the general direction and control. Experience, to be brief, has shown me that in founding a journal wherein my interest should not be merely editorial, lies my sole chance of carrying out to completion whatever peculiar intentions I may have entertained."

Despite the wide diffusion of the prospectus containing these paragraphs, and the exertions of the poet, a sufficient number of subscribers to start the projected publication on a sound basis could not be obtained, and the scheme fell through, or, rather, was deferred for a time. It has been stated that some numbers of *The Stylus* were, indeed, published ; but this assertion, it is believed, was only founded on the fact of a " dummy " copy having been printed as a specimen of what it was intended to offer the public.

Notwithstanding the failure of the magazine project, Mr. Clarke and Poe remained on a very amicable footing, the former doing all his limited powers permitted to befriend the latter, and assist him in his literary plans. In a vindication of the poet from the slanders of his first biographer, Mr. Clarke says, with reference to " Poe and the wife he so tenderly loved . . . I have some singular revelations which throw a strong light on the causes that darkened the life, and made most unhappy the death, of one of the most remarkable of all our literary men." " During his engagement in my office," continues this authority, " I published a life of Mr. Poe, with a portrait from a daguerreotype. Both the life and the portrait are utterly unlike the gross caricatures manufactured since his death ; . . . the portrait prefixed to a recent volume of Poe's poems bears no resemblance to the fine, intellectual head of Poe." "Why," indignantly demands Mr. Clarke —"why are such wrongs perpetrated upon the dead ? why are they permitted ? " The life published by Mr. Clarke is stated by Griswold to have been prepared "in Philadelphia, in 1843," by Poe himself, for a paper called *The Museum*, and he pretends to quote from it in order to prove that "many parts of it are untrue." The second paragraph is assumed to be a citation from a letter of Miss Barrett (Mrs. Browning), referring to "The Raven," a poem *not then written*, much less published !

During 1843 Poe·continued contributing, chiefly critiques, to *Graham's Magazine*. Amongst other writings he completed the tale of "The Gold Bug," and sold it to Mr. Graham for fifty-two dollars. *The Dollar* newspaper, a publication edited by N. P. Willis, offering a premium of \$100 for the best tale, Poe obtained his manuscript back from Mr. Graham, submitted it to the adjudicators, and, for it, was awarded the prize. The history of this practical illustration of the poet's cipher theory that human ingenuity cannot construct an enigma human ingenuity cannot resolve, is a further proof of the frequent inability of publishers to gauge the pecuniary value of literary works. In an unpublished letter, Poe, referring to this—in America—most popular of his productions, says, "'The Gold Bug' was originally sent to Graham; but he not liking it, I got him to take some critical papers instead, and sent it to 'The Dollar Newspaper,' which had offered $100 for the best story. It obtained the premium, and made a great noise."

This tale, although founded upon trite and threadbare worn incidents, has an air of freshness and originality from the novelty of the scientific theory by which it is permeated: Poe may not have been the first to discover, but he certainly was the first to popularise, the discovery of the mathematical ratio in which the letters of the alphabet recur. In enshrining this technicality in the story of a hidden treasure, he adopted the very best method of fascinating the attention " of the greatest number." In his two favourite and, *apparently*, contradictory styles of art, simplicity and suggestiveness, this tale is decidedly its author's *chef d'œuvre*.

Despite the timely aid of the one hundred dollar prize, Poe's pecuniary affairs appear to have reached a very trying stage by this period, and nothing but incessant labour enabled him to keep himself and family from utter destitution. For *The Pioneer*, a monthly magazine edited by Mr. J. R. Lowell, and

which Poe says "was an excellent work, but had
a *very* limited circulation," he wrote some reviews,
including one on one of Griswold's compilations, the
principal paragraphs of which were subsequently
embodied in an article on the " Rationale of Verse."
During the year he also contributed various critiques to
*Graham's Magazine* on " Channing " (a nephew of Dr.
Channing), " Halleck," " Cooper," and other somewhat
forgotten celebrities.    In his article on Channing
Poe thus alluded to Tennyson, a not very "popular "
poet at that time :—

" For Tennyson, as for a man imbued with the richest and
rarest poetic impulses, we have an admiration—a reverence
unbounded.    His ' Morte d'Arthur,' his ' Locksley Hall,' his
' Sleeping Beauty,' his ' Lady of Shalott,' his ' Lotos Eaters,'
his ' Œnone,' and many other poems, are not surpassed, in all
that gives to Poetry its distinctive value, by the compositions
of any one living or dead.    And his leading error—that error
which renders him unpopular—a point, to be sure, of no particular importance—that very error, we say, is founded in
truth—in a keen perception of the elements of poetic beauty.
We allude to his quaintness—to what the world chooses to
term his affectation.    No true poet—no critic whose approbation is worth even a copy of the volume we now hold in
our hand—will deny that he feels impressed, sometimes even
to tears, by many of those very affectations which he is
impelled by the prejudice of his education, or by the cant of
his reason, to condemn.    He should thus be led to examine
the extent of the one, and to be wary of the deductions of
the other.    In fact, the profound intuition of Lord Bacon has

supplied. in one of his immortal apothegms, the whole philosophy of the point at issue. 'There is no exquisite beauty,'
he truly says, 'without some *strangeness* in its proportions.'
We maintain, then, that Tennyson errs, not in his occasional
quaintness, but in its continual and obtrusive excess. And,
in accusing Mr. Channing of having been inoculated with
*virus* from Tennyson, we merely mean to say that he has
adopted and exaggerated that noble poet's characteristic
defect, having mistaken it for his principal merit!"

The article on "Fitz-Greene Halleck" contained
some very pertinent remarks on the adventitious
reputations acquired by the pioneers of a country's
literature. "Those rank first who were first known,"
declares Poe, adding that among the literary pioneers
of America "there is not one whose productions have
not been grossly overrated by his countrymen." Such
home truths were scarcely calculated to gain the poet
"golden opinions" from his contemporaries, nor increase
his popularity with his brother journalists. But he
dared all *published* opinion, and in the very teeth of
Cooper's supreme popularity ventured upon saying, in
reviewing one of that author's forest stories :—

"The interest, as usual, has no reference to *plot*, of which,
indeed, our novelist seems altogether regardless, or incapable ;
but depends, first, upon the nature of the theme ; secondly,
upon a Robinson-Crusoe-like detail in its management ; and
thirdly, upon the frequently repeated portraiture of the half-
civilised Indian. In saying that the interest depends, first,
upon the nature of the theme, we mean to suggest that this

theme—life in the wilderness—is one of intrinsic and universal interest, appealing to the heart of man in all phases; a
theme, like that of life upon the ocean, so unfailingly omniprevalent in its power of arresting and absorbing attention,
that while success or popularity is, with such a subject,
expected as a matter of course, a failure might be properly
regarded as conclusive evidence of imbecility on the part of
the author. The two theses in question have been handled
*usque ad nauseam*—and this through the instinctive perception of the universal interest which appertains to them. A
writer, distrustful of his powers, can scarcely do better than
discuss either one or the other. A man of genius will rarely,
and should never, undertake either; first, because both are
excessively hackneyed; and, secondly, because the reader
never fails, in forming his opinion of a book, to make dis-
count, either wittingly or unwittingly, for that intrinsic interest which is inseparable from the subject and independent of
the manner in which it is treated. Very few, and very dull
indeed, are those who do not instantaneously perceive the distinction; and thus there are two great classes of fictions—a
popular and widely-circulated class, read with pleasure, but
without admiration—in which the author is lost or forgotten;
or remembered, if at all, with something very nearly akin to
contempt; and then, a class, not so popular, nor so widely
diffused, in which, at every paragraph, arises a distinctive and
highly pleasurable interest, springing from our perception and
appreciation of the skill employed, or the genius evinced in
the composition. After perusal of the one class, we think
solely of the book; after reading the other, chiefly of the
author. The former class leads to popularity; the latter to
fame. In the former case, the books sometimes live, while
the authors usually die; in the latter, even when the works

perish, the man survives. Among American writers of the less generally circulated, but more worthy and more artistic fictions, we may mention Mr. Brockden Brown, Mr. John Neal, Mr. Simms, Mr. Hawthorne; at the head of the more popular division we may place Mr. Cooper."

These caustic critiques notwithstanding, Poe's literary labours for 1843 and the following year, taken altogether, were poorer in quality and quantity, and, doubtless, in remuneration, than in any succeeding, or preceding, year since his first adoption of literature as a profession. But these years were, it must be remembered, those in which the poet was first awakened to the fell certainty of his darling wife's mortal illness— the dreadful years in which he first really succumbed to the temptations of temporary oblivion proffered by drugs and stimulants.

In speaking of the "quantity" of his writings referable to this melancholy epoch of the poet's career, *original* matter only must be considered as alluded to. In his mental incapacity to produce anything of his own, Poe appears to have resorted to translating from the French. From April 1843, until the beginning of 1845, a constant, an almost weekly, supply of translated tales and sketches appear over his initials in the pages of the New York *New Mirror*, and its successor, the *Evening Mirror*. This bread-and-butter work, executed under high pressure, must have been a most terrible infliction for Poe's morbidly sensitive temperament, and, despite the few reviews taken by *Graham's*, have barely sufficed to maintain the unfortunate man and his household above veritable starvation. Among the various schemes he endeavoured to plan during his leisure—his lucid—intervals, was the republication of his tales in periodic parts, but we have no evidence that anything more appeared than number one of "The Prose Romances of Edgar A. Poe," containing "The Murders in the Rue Morgue," and "The Man that was Used Up."

In the winter of 1843, he delivered a lecture at the "William Wirt" Institution, on the "Poets and Poetry of America," and, in the course of the evening, took occasion to deliver some very severe remarks upon Mr. Griswold's compilation, recently published under a title similar to that given by Poe to his discourse. This trenchant attack upon the new and much belauded volume created no little excitement at the time in the literary coteries of Philadelphia, and by the book's compiler was never forgiven, and was terribly avenged. Mr. Griswold, it should be mentioned, for a short time occupied the editorial chair in Mr. Graham's publishing office which Poe had vacated. To the March number of *Graham's Magazine* Poe contributed a lengthy and appreciative review of Horne's magnificent epic, "Orion." Criticism was scarcely the poet's *forte;* and although the instincts of his own genius invariably prompted him to recognise and acknowledge the productions of kindred spirits, his critiques more closely resemble the unravelling an intricate riddle, than the sympathetic or antipathetic discussion of a propounded subject. And yet when we peruse Poe's definition of the rules of Art—as furnished by Nature—we cannot refuse to acknowledge their truth. Some of his more remarkable utterances in this review of "Orion," as embodying the theories he believed, and strove to follow out in poesy, may be reproduced here : —

"Although we agree, for example, with Coleridge, that poetry and *passion* are discordant, yet we are willing to permit Tennyson to bring to the intense *passion* which prompted his 'Locksley Hall,' the aid of that terseness and pungency which are derivable from rhythm and from rhyme. The effect he produces, however, is a purely passionate, and not, unless in detached passages of this magnificent philippic, a properly poetic effect. His 'Œnone,' on the other hand, exalts the soul not into passion, but into a conception of pure *beauty,* which in its elevation—its calm and intense rapture—has in it a foreshadowing of the future and spiritual life, and as far transcends earthly passion as the holy radiance of the sun does the glimmering and feeble phosphorescence of the glow-worm. His 'Morte d'Arthur' is in the same majestic vein. The 'Sensitive Plant' of Shelley is in the same sublime spirit. Nor, if the passionate poems of Byron excite more intensely a greater number of readers than either the 'Œnone,' or the

'Sensitive Plant,' does this indisputable fact prove anything more than that the majority of mankind are more susceptible of the impulses of passion than of the impressions of beauty? Readers do exist, however, and always will exist, who, to hearts of maddening fervour, unite in perfection the sentiment of the beautiful—that divine sixth sense which is yet so faintly understood—that sense which phrenology has attempted to embody in its organ of *ideality*—that sense which is the basis of all Cousin's dreams—that sense which speaks of GOD through His purest, if not His *sole* attribute—which proves, and which alone proves His existence.

" To readers such as these—and only to such as these— must be left the decision of what the true Poesy is. And these—with *no* hesitation—will decide that the origin of Poetry lies in a thirst for a wilder Beauty than Earth supplies —that Poetry itself is the imperfect effort to quench this immortal thirst by novel combinations of beautiful forms (collocations of forms), physical or spiritual, and that this thirst when even partially allayed—this sentiment when even feebly meeting response—produces emotion to which all other human emotions are vapid and insignificant.

" We shall now be fully understood. If, with Coleridge, and, however erring at times, his was precisely the mind fitted to decide a question such as this—if, with him, we reject *passion* from the true—from the pure poetry—if we reject even passion—if we discard as feeble, as unworthy the high spirituality of the theme (which has its origin in a sense of the Godhead), if we dismiss even the nearly divine emotion of human *love*—that emotion which, merely to name, causes the pen to tremble—with how much greater reason shall we dismiss all else? And yet there are men who would mingle with the august theme the merest questions of expediency—

the cant topics of the day—the doggerel æsthetics of the time—who would trammel the soul in its flight to an ideal Ilelusion, by the quirks and quibbles of chopped logic. There are men who do this—lately there are a set of men who make a practice of doing this—and who defend it on the score of the advancement of what they suppose to be *truth.* Truth is, in its own essence, sublime; but her loftiest sublimity, as derived from man's clouded and erratic reason, is valueless— is pulseless—is utterly ineffective when brought into comparison with the unerring *sense* of which we speak; yet grant this *truth* to be all which its seekers and worshippers pretend— they forget that it is not truth, *per se,* which is made their thesis, but an *argumentation,* often maudlin and pedantic, always shallow and unsatisfactory (as from the mere inadaptation of the vehicle it *must* be) by which this *truth,* in casual and indeterminate glimpses, is, *or is not,* rendered manifest."

After pointing out the matters in which he deemed Horne had departed from the proper standard—the standard which he, Poe, assumed to be the true one— he concluded by acknowledging that "Orion" "will be admitted by every man of genius to be one of the noblest, if not the very noblest, poetical works of the age. Its defects are trivial and conventional; its beauties intrinsic and supreme."

Consequent, apparently, upon this critique, some correspondence took place between the two poets. " During a certain period of Poe's * troubled circum-

* Edgar Allan Poe. A Memorial Volume. Baltimore, 1877, pp. 82, 83.

stances," writes Horne, " he wrote to me, I being then
in London, and inclosed a manuscript, saying that he
had singled me out, though personally a stranger, to
ask the friendly service of handing a certain story to
the editor of one of the magazines, with a view, of
course, to some remittance.   Without waiting to read
the story I replied at once that I considered his
application to me a great compliment, and that I would
certainly do the best I could in the business.   But
when I read the story, my heart of hope sank within
me : it was ' The Spectacles.'  I tried several magazines,
not an editor would touch it.   In vain I represented
the remarkable tact with which the old lady, under
the very trying task she had set herself, did, nevertheless, maintain her female delicacy and dignity.   I met
with nothing beyond a deaf ear, an uplifted eyebrow,
or the ejaculations of a gentleman pretending to feel
quite shocked.   It may be that false modesty, and
social, as well as religious, hypocrisy, are the con-
comitant and counterpart of our present equivocal
state of civilisation; but if I were not an Englishman,
it is more than probable I should say that those
qualities were more glaringly conspicuous in England
than in any other country."   No comment is needed
here upon the fact that any imagination could be discovered so ultraprurient, and utterly ridiculous, as to
perceive anything contrary to the most rigid and puri-

tanic delicacy in the playful, but not very powerful, *badinage* of " The Spectacles."

One day in April of this year, 1844, the good folks of New York were startled by a *jeu d'esprit*, or hoax, on the subject of Ballooning, and Poe was the author. The *Sun*, in which this amusing sally appeared, had already a reputation for information not elsewhere obtainable, in consequence of its publication of the notorious " Moon Hoax " article,\* when one morning its readers—and their number increased that day with much celerity—were astounded by reading the following wonderful communication :—

" ASTOUNDING NEWS BY EXPRESS, *via* NORFOLK !

" THE ATLANTIC CROSSED IN THREE DAYS !!

"SIGNAL TRIUMPH OF Mr. MONCK MASON'S FLYING MACHINE !!!

" *Arrival at Sullivan's Island, near Charleston, S.C., of Mr. Mason, Mr. Robert Holland, Mr. Henson, Mr. Harrison Ainsworth, and four others, in the Steering Balloon, ' Victoria,' after a passage of seventy-five hours from Land to Land ! Full Particulars of the Voyage !* "

This wonderful record of unparalleled adventure was originally published, as its concocter, indeed, confessed, " with the preceding heading in magnificent capitals, well interspersed with notes of admiration, as a matter of fact, in the *New York Sun*, a daily

\* *Vide* pp. 119–123.

newspaper, and therein fully subserved the purpose of creating indigestible aliment for the *quidnuncs* during the few hours intervening between a couple of the Charleston mails. The rush for the 'sole paper which had the news' was something beyond even the prodigious; and, in fact, if (as some assert) the 'Victoria' *did* not absolutely accomplish the voyage recorded, it will be difficult to assign a reason why she *should* not have accomplished it."

As a *jeu d'esprit*, this trick on public credulity was a splendid success, but such jests are scarcely the class of productions one would desire to obtain from a poetic genius. Doubtless, for the immediate needs of the hour, these clever impositions paid their author much better than did the best of his poems, whilst they also furnished more ample food for his cravings for reputation, and his insatiable love of hoaxing. Poe's readers and admirers must, in point of fact, always be upon their guard against his inveterate habit of attempting to gauge their gullibility; his passion for this propensity frequently led him into indulging in the practice when least expected—into giving way to the desire of befooling his readers when apparently most in earnest.

In the same month as "The Balloon Hoax," Godey published in his *Lady's Book*, a literary magazine of Philadelphia, "A Tale of the Ragged Mountains." It was one of its author's favourite stories, and the scene

of it is laid in the vicinity where his college days were
spent, that is to say, in the neighbourhood of Charlottesville. Taken in connection with mesmeric
theories—and at this period Poe appears to have been
investigating such theories with the most steadfast
interest—this tale is a singular manifestation, but,
beyond some Poësque *traits* of thought and diction,
contains nothing very remarkable. The Death Fetch,
Doppelgänger, and similar dual creations of superstition
have always been numerous enough in literature, and
this revivification, although treated in a suggestively
original manner, calls for no lengthy comment. Perhaps, when Poe's own habits are considered, and his
love of mystification fully allowed for, the most interesting passages in the tale will be found in these
allusions to its hero's use of drugs :—" His imagination
was singularly vigorous and creative ; and no doubt it
derived additional force from the habitual use of
morphine, which he swallowed in great quantity, and
without which he would have found it impossible to
exist. It was his practice to take a very large dose
of it immediately after breakfast each morning—or
rather, immediately after a cup of strong coffee, for he
ate nothing in the forenoon—and then set forth alone,
or attended only by a dog, upon a long ramble. , . .
In the meantime," that is to say, after some hours
walking, " the morphine had its customary effect—

that of enduing all the external world with an intensity
of interest. In the quivering of a leaf—in the hue
of a blade of grass—in the shape of a trefoil—in the
humming of a bee—in the gleaming of a dewdrop—
in the breathing of the wind—in the faint odours that
came from the forest—there came a whole universe
of suggestion—a gay and motley train of rhapsodical
and immethodical thought."

Scarcely any original composition is again discernible until the end of the year. A review, already
alluded to, in *The Pioneer*, and the quaintly beautiful
verses, "Dreamland," published in the June number
of *Graham's*, are all we can trace before the following
September. The poem is replete with words—thoughts
—expressions—that have appeared again, and again,
in others of their author's poems, but is, nevertheless,
most idiosyncratic and original. Those who have thus
far followed Poe's "route, obscure and lonely," need
not ask who is "the traveller" that

> " Meets aghast
> Sheeted Memories of the Past—
> Shrouded forms that start and sigh
> As they pass the wanderer by—
> White-robed forms of friends long given,
> In agony, to the Earth—and Heaven."

"The Oblong Box" appeared in Godey's *Lady's
Book* for September. It is a tale of no particular merit,

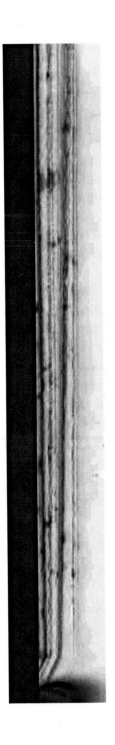

for Poe, and is chiefly remarkable for some s
curious mental analyses.   In this same m<
*New Mirror* perished, and with it, of course,
fortunate poet's chief, although slender, s
livelihood.  Thoroughly adrift, something dec
now to be done, and done at once.   A living
to be had, apparently, from literature in Phil
and the conclusion was arrived at, probably
some intimation from Willis, to seek New Y
more.

## CHAPTER XIV.

### *NEW YORK ONCE MORE.*

EDGAR POE'S reputation had already preceded him to
New York, where, indeed, the publications of N. P.
Willis, and other literary correspondents and friends,
had kept his name for some time before the public.

 " Our first knowledge of Mr. Poe's removal to this
city," says Willis, * " was by a call which we received
from a lady who introduced herself to us as the
mother of his wife.   She was in search of employment
for him, and she excused her errand by mentioning
that he was ill, that her daughter was a confirmed
invalid, and that their circumstances were such as
compelled her taking it upon herself.   The countenance of this lady, made beautiful and saintly by an
evidently complete giving up of her life to privation
and sorrowful tenderness, her gentle and mournful
voice urging its plea, her long-forgotten but habitually
and unconsciously refined manners, and her appealing
yet appreciative mention of the claims and abilities of

* *Home Journal*, Saturday, October 13, 1849.

her son, disclosed at once the presence of one of those
angels upon earth that women in adversity can be.
It was a hard fate that she was watching over. Mr.
Poe wrote with fastidious difficulty, and in a style too
much above the popular level to be well paid. He
was always in pecuniary difficulty, and, with his sick
wife, frequently in want of the merest necessities of
life."

The immediate result of that interview with Mrs.
Clemm is not told; but, eventually, Edgar Poe was
engaged as sub-editor on the *Evening Mirror.* Willis,
writing to his former partner Morris, * when called
upon to make some remarks respecting his acquaintance with the deceased poet, says, in language that
would give greater gratification were it a little less
self-glorifying :—

"In our harassing and exhausting days of ' daily ' editorship, Poe, *for a long time*, was our assistant—the constant and
industrious occupant of a desk in our office. . . . Poe came
to us quite incidentally, neither of us having been *personally*
acquainted with him till that time ; and his position towards
us, and connection with us, of course unaffected by claims of
previous friendship, were a fair average of his general intercourse and impressions. As he was a man who never smiled,
and never said a propitiatory or deprecating word, we were
not likely to have been seized with any sudden partiality or
wayward caprice in his favour.

---

* From Idlewild, October 17, 1859.

"*I should* preface my avowal of an *almost reverence* for the man, as I knew him, by reminding the reader of the strange double, common to the presence and magnetism of a man of genius, the mysterious electricity of mind. . . .

"It was rather a step downward, after being the chief editor of several monthlies, as Poe had been, to come into the office of a daily journal as a mechanical paragraphist. It was his business to sit at a desk, in a corner of the editorial room, ready to be called upon for any of the miscellaneous work of the day ; yet you remember how absolutely and how good-humouredly ready he was for any suggestion; how punctually and industriously reliable in the following out of the wish once expressed ; how cheerful and present-minded his work when he might excusably have been so listless and abstracted. *We loved the man* for the entireness of fidelity with which he served us. When he left us, we were very reluctant to part with him."

Again, in the letter to the *Home Journal* already referred to, Willis says :—

"Poe was employed by us, for several months, as critic and sub-editor. This was our first personal acquaintance with him. He resided with his wife and mother at Fordham,* a few miles out of town, but was at his desk in the office from nine in the morning till the evening paper went to press. With the highest admiration for his genius, and a willingness to let it atone for more than ordinary irregularity, we were led by common report to expect a very capricious attention to his duties, and, occasionally, a scene of

* This is a mistake : Poe did not remove to Fordham until 1846.
—J. H. I.

violence and difficulty.  Time went on, however, and he was invariably punctual and industrious.   With his pale, beautiful, and intellectual face, as a reminder of what genius was in him, it was impossible, of course, not to treat him always with deferential courtesy, and, to our occasional request that he would not probe too deep in a criticism, or that he would erase a passage coloured too highly with his resentments against society and mankind, he readily and courteously assented—far more yielding than most men, we thought, on points so excusably sensitive.   With a prospect of taking the lead in another periodical, he, at last, voluntarily gave up his employment with us, and, through all this considerable period, we had seen but one presentment of the man—a quiet, patient, industrious, and most gentlemanly person, commanding the utmost respect and good feeling by his unvarying deportment and ability."

This characterisation of the poet is not of much importance, save that it affords another link in the chain of evidence as to Poe's general behaviour.   Mr. Willis's fondness for patronising his betters is somewhat ludicrous, and he quite forgets to remark that the profits of his grandiloquent paper scarcely sufficed to pay *his* "critic and sub-editor" an *honorarium* large enough to keep body and spirit together.   Poe's contributions to the *Evening Mirror* were not great either in quality or quantity, and soon after his resignation of his post upon it, the paper passed from Messrs. Willis and Morris into the hands of new proprietors.   At first, beyond those of a "mechanical paragraphist," Poe's duties in his new position had not called for much activity. In October he appears to have resumed his translations from the French, and to have continued them in the columns of this paper for several months, but it is not until the beginning of the following January that any original writing therein can be traced to his pen.

Meanwhile, in Godey's magazine for November, was published his tale, "Thou Art the Man,"—one of the most conventional of his fictions ; and in the *Southern Literary Messenger* for December, a caustic satire on the "Mutual Admiration Society" system among editors, entitled "The Literary Life of Thingum Bob, Esq., late Editor of the *Goosetherumfoodle*." More important than these were the initial papers of "Marginalia," contributed to the *Democratic Review*, during the last two months of the year. From the introduction to these pungent, pithy, paragraphs, which were continued in the pages of various publications up to the very day of their author's death, and which, despite their idiosyncratic powers, have not yet all been collected — these sentences may be fittingly reproduced :—

"In getting my books I have been always solicitous of an ample margin ; this not so much through any love of the thing in itself, however agreeable, as for the facility it affords me of pencilling suggested thoughts, agreements, and differences of opinion, or brief critical comments in general. Where what I have to note is too much to be included within the narrow limits of a margin, I commit it to a slip of paper, and deposit it between the leaves; taking care to secure it by an imperceptible portion of gum tragacanth paste.

"All this may be whim; it may be not only a very hackneyed, but a very idle practice, yet I persist in it still; and it affords me pleasure—which is profit, in despite of Mr. Bentham with Mr. Mill on his back.

"This making of notes, however, is by no means the making of mere *memoranda*—a custom which has its disadvantages, beyond doubt. '*Ce que je mets sur papier,*' says Bernardin de St. Pierre, '*je remets de ma mémoire, et par consequence je l'oublie;*' and, in fact, if you wish to forget anything on the spot, make a note that this thing is to be remembered.

"But the purely marginal jottings, done with no eye to the Memorandum Book, have a distinct complexion, and not only a distinct purpose, but none at all; this it is which imparts to them a value. They have a rank somewhat above the chance and desultory comments of literary chit-chat—for these latter are not unfrequently 'talk for talk's sake,' hurried out of the mouth; while the *marginalia* are deliberately pencilled, because the mind of the reader wishes to unburthen itself of a *thought*—however flippant—however silly—however trivial—still a thought indeed, not merely a thing that might have been a thought in time, and under more favourable circumstances. In the *marginalia*, too, we talk only to ourselves; we therefore talk freshly—boldly—originally—with *abandonnement* — without conceit — much after the fashion of Jeremy Taylor, and Sir Thomas Browne, and Sir William Temple, and the anatomical Burton, and that most

logical analogist Butler, and some other people of the old day,
who were too full of their matter to have any room for their
manner, which being thus left out of question was a capital
manner indeed—a model of manners, with a richly marginallic
air. The circumscription of space, too, in these pencillings,
has in it something more of advantage than inconvenience.
It compels us (whatever diffuseness of idea we may clandes-
tinely entertain) into Montesquieu-ism, into Tacitus-ism
(here I leave out of view the concluding portion of the
' Annals '). . . . .

"During a rainy afternoon, not long ago, being in a mood
too listless for continuous study, I sought relief from *ennui* in
dipping here and there at random among the volumes of my
library—no very large one certainly, but sufficiently miscellaneous, and, I flatter myself, not a little *recherché*.

" Perhaps it was what the Germans call the ' brain-scatter-
ing' humour of the moment ; but, while the picturesqueness
of the numerous pencil-scratches arrested my attention, their
helter-skelteriness of commentary amused me. I found myself at length forming a wish that it had been some other
hand than my own which had so bedevilled the books, and
fancying that, in such case, I might have derived no inconsiderable pleasure from turning them over. From this the
transition-thought (as Mr. Lyell, or Mr. Murchison, or Mr.
Featherstonhaugh would have it) was natural enough—there
might be something even in *my* scribblings which, for the
mere sake of scribbling, would have interest for others.

" The main difficulty respected the mode of transferring the
notes from the volumes—the context from the text—without
detriment to that exceedingly frail fabric of intelligibility in
which the context was imbedded. With all appliances to
boot, with the printed pages at their back, the commentaries

were too often like Dodona's oracles—or those of Lycophron
Tenebrosus—or the essays of the pedant's pupils in Quintillian,
which were 'necessarily excellent, since even he (the pedant)
found it impossible to comprehend them : ' what, then, would
become of it—this context—if transferred—if translated ?
Would it not rather be *traduit* (traduced) which is the French
synonyme, or *overzezet* (turned topsy-turvy) which is the
Dutch one ?

"I concluded at length to put extensive faith in the acumen
and imagination of the reader—this as a general rule.   But,
in some instances, where even faith would not remove mountains, there seemed no safer plan than so to remodel the note
as to convey at least the ghost of a conception as to what it
was all about.   Where, for such conception, the text itself
was absolutely necessary, I could quote it ; where the title of
the book commented upon was indispensable, I could name
it.   In short, like a novel-hero dilemma'd, I made up my mind
' to be guided by circumstances,' in default of more satisfactory rules of conduct.

"As for the multitudinous opinion expressed in the sub-
joined *farrago*—as for my present assent to all, or dissent
from any portion of it—as to the possibility of my having in
some instances altered my mind—or as to the impossibility
of my not having altered it often—these are points upon
which I say nothing, because upon these there can be nothing
cleverly said.   It may be as well to observe, however, that
just as the goodness of your true pun is in the direct ratio of
its intolerability, so is nonsense the essential sense of the
Marginal Note."

Following this introduction are various specimens
of Poe's ideas, grave and gay, on all kinds of topics.

The puns and jests are no better than such light ware is generally, but his opinions on certain books and their authors, and on some of the arts and sciences, deserve preservation. Music is a frequent theme with him, for of music he was a passionate devotee, and a capable student. Speaking in commendatory terms of the late H. F. Chorley, he says, " But the philosophy of music is beyond his depth, and of its physics he, unquestionably, has no conception. By the way," he adds, " of all the so-called scientific musicians, how many may we suppose cognisant of the acoustic facts and mathematical deductions ? To be sure, my acquaintance with eminent composers is quite limited ; but I have never met *one* who did not stare and say 'yes,' 'no,' 'hum !' 'ha !' 'eh ?' when I mentioned the mechanism of the *Siréne,* or made allusion to the oval vibrations at right angles."

A lengthy note is devoted to a presumed omission in all the Bridgewater treatises, in their failure to notice " *the great* idiosyncrasy in the Divine system of adaptation — that idiosyncrasy which stamps the adaptation as Divine, in distinction from that which is the work of merely human constructiveness. I speak," he asserts, " of the complete *mutuality* of adaptation," and then proceeds to furnish examples, needless to cite here, concluding in drawing a contrast between human and divine inventions,

" the plots of God are perfect. The Universe is a plot of God."

Referring to his favourite author, Dickens, he remarks that his " serious (minor) compositions have been lost in the blaze of his comic reputation. One of the most forcible things ever written," he opines, " is a short story of his, called ' The Black Veil ; ' a strangely-pathetic and richly-imaginative production, replete with the loftiest tragic power." That Dickens's head must puzzle the phrenologists then occurs to him, for in it, he observes, " the organs of ideality are small ; and the conclusion of the ' Curiosity Shop ' is more truly ideal (in both phrenological senses) than any composition of equal length in the English language."

Some ideas are then hazarded as to the treatment to be awarded dunces ; " where the gentler sex is concerned," says the chivalrous poet, " there seems but one course for the critic—speak if you can commend ; be silent, if not." Frequently his opinions run counter to those of the immense majority of his republican brethren, as in the note, " The sense of high birth is a moral force whose value the democrats are never in condition to calculate : ' *Pour savoir ce qu'est Dieu,*' says the Baron de Bielfeld, ' *il faut être Dieu même.*' " His views and reviews of things in general, as set forth in these original and entertaining Marginalia, supply ample literary food for interest and imagination, but scarcely need lengthy notice in their author's biography, albeit they open many unsuspected sidelights upon the darker recesses of his mental story. When, for instance, he declares " I am far more than half-serious in all that I have ever said about manuscript, as affording indication of character," we feel that he is really confiding in us, as also in the sequence, " I by no means shrink from acknowledging that I act, hourly, upon estimates of character derived from chirography." " How many good books suffer neglect through the inefficiency of their beginnings," is a thought, indeed, likely to have been in the mind of him who invariably acts up to his advice here given, of " at all risks, let there be a few vivid sentences, *imprimis*, by way of the electric bell to the telegraph." A large portion of his misfortunes—the rôle of critic he was compelled to play being really compulsory— are suggested by the assertion that "a man of genius, if not permitted to choose his own subject, will do worse, in letters, than if he had talents none at all. And *here* how imperatively is he controlled!" " To be sure!" exclaimed Poe, " he can write to suit himself, but in the same manner his publishers print." Whilst the accusation in the following paragraph is too surely pointed to be taken for any one else than self-reference : —" It is the curse of a certain order of mind, that it

can never rest satisfied with the consciousness of its
ability to do a thing. Still less is it content with
doing it. It must both know and show how it was
done."

With 1845 was inaugurated the most brilliant
epoch of Poe's literary career, although the continually
increasing weakness of his wife flung a cloud of gloom
over its brightness. In *The Gift* for the new year
appeared " The Purloined Letter," the last of the famous
detective trilogy, of which the " Rue Morgue " and
" Marie Roget " mysteries form parts. The three tales
should always be read in conjunction with one another,
because, although published separately, and each complete in itself, the one is but a sequence of the analytic
reasoning of the other, and all are but varied examples
of the futility of over acuteness, or rather cunning,
when opposed by extraordinary combinations, or by
the calculations of genius.

On January 4th was published the first number
of a new periodical, entitled *The Broadway Journal.*
" It was not until No. 10 that I had anything to do
with this journal as editor," is Poe's endorsement upon
our copy, but from its commencement he wrote for it.
To the first, and the following number, he contributed a
review of Mrs. Browning's " Drama of Exile and other
Poems," and, whilst not forgetful of his critical seve-
rities, he found enough in the work to call forth his

most enthusiastic admiration and poetic sympathy.
That she had, even then, done more in poetry than
any woman, living or dead, was a decision Poe could
not fail to arrive at; neither was he singular nor original
in deeming that she had " surpassed all her poetical
contemporaries of either sex, with a single exception,"
that exception being Tennyson. What Mrs. Browning
thought of her transatlantic reviewer's strictures on her
presumed want of due knowledge of the mechanism of
verse may be gathered from this extract out of a letter
to Mr. Horne :—

"Mr. Poe seems to me in a great mist on the subject of
metre. You yourself have skipped all the philosophy of the
subject in your excellent treatise on 'Chaucer Modernised,'
and you shut your ears when I tried to dun you about it one
day. But Chaucer wrote on precisely the same principles
(eternal principles) as the Greek poets did, I believe, unalter-
ably; and you, who are a musician, ought to have sung it
out loud in the ears of the public. There is no 'pedantic
verbiage' in Longinus. But Mr. Poe, who attributes the
'Œdipus Colonœus' to Æschylus (*vide* review on me), sits
somewhat loosely, probably, on his classics."

Poe, certainly, was not a profound Greek scholar;
but he had been to classical schools, and was a well-
read man, and could not, therefore, have ascribed the
Sophoclesian drama to Æschylus, save in a fit of
oblivious haste, such as, indeed, the somewhat in-

volved nature of the passage in question suggests must
have been the case in this instance.

A critique on N. P. Willis constituted Poe's sole contribution to the third number of the *Broadway Journal*,
and it contained nothing very original or striking, but
was chiefly occupied by an elaborate discussion as to the
boundaries between Fancy and Imagination, travelling
over much the same ground that had been traversed
five years previously, in a review of Moore's poetry.

On the 29th of January the first published version
of Poe's poetic *chef d'œuvre*, the far-famed " Raven,"
appeared in the *Evening Mirror*, with these introductory
words by Willis :—

" We are permitted to copy, (in advance of publication,)
from the second No. of the *American Review*, the following
remarkable poem by Edgar Poe.  In our opinion, it is the
most effective single example of ' fugitive poetry ' ever published in this country ; and unsurpassed in English poetry
for subtle conception, masterly ingenuity of versification, and
consistent sustaining of imaginative lift. . . . It is one of
those ' dainties bred in a book,' which we feed on.  It will
stick to the memory of everybody who reads it."

This publication with the author's name, and the
immediate reproduction of the poem in the journals
of nearly every town in the United States, prevented
any attempt at concealment, had Poe really thought to
make one.  Certain it is that " The Raven " appeared

in the *American Review* for February, as by " Quarles,"
preceded by the following note, the inspiration, evidently, of the poet himself :—

" The following lines from a correspondent, besides the
deep quaint strain of the sentiment, and the curious introduction of some ludicrous touches amidst the serious and impressive, as was doubtless intended by the author—appear to
us one of the most felicitous specimens of unique rhyming
which has for some time met our eye. The resources of
English rhythm for varieties of melody, measure, and sound,
producing corresponding diversities of effect, have been
thoroughly studied, much more perceived, by very few poets
in the language. While the classic tongues, especially the
Greek, possess, by power of accent, several advantages for
versification over our own, chiefly through greater abundance
of spondaic feet, we have other, and very great advantages of
sound, by the modern usage of rhyme. Alliteration is nearly
the only effect of that kind which the ancients had in common
with us. It will be seen that much of the melody of " The
Raven " arises from alliteration, and the studious use of similar sounds in unusual places. In regard to its measure, it
may be noted, that if all the verses were like the second, they
might properly be placed merely in short lines, producing a
not uncommon form ; but the presence in all the others of
one line—mostly the second in the verse—which flows con-
tinuously, with *only* an aspirate pause in the middle, like
that before the short line in the Sapphic Adonic, while the
fifth has at the middle pause no similarity of sound with any
part beside, give the versification an entirely different effect.
We could wish the capacities of our noble language, in
prosody, were better understood."

No single "fugitive" poem ever caused such a *furor ;* in the course of a few weeks it spread over the whole of the United States, calling into existence parodies and imitations innumerable, and, indeed, creating quite a literature of its own ; it carried its author's name and fame from shore to shore, inducing veritable poets in other lands——last but not least, Monsieur Mallarmè, —— to attempt to transmute its magical charms into their tongues ; it drew admiring testimony from some of the finest spirits of the age, and, finally, made Poe the lion of the season. And for this masterpiece of genius—this poem which has, probably, done more for the renown of American letters than any other single work—it is alleged that Poe, then in the heyday of his intellect and reputation, received the sum of *ten* dollars !

Mrs. Browning, then Miss Barrett, in a letter written some time after publication of this poem, says : "This vivid writing !—this power *which* is felt ! 'The Raven' has produced a sensation—a 'fit horror' here in England. Some of my friends are taken by the fear of it, and some by the music. I hear of persons *haunted* by the Nevermore, and one acquaintance of mine, who has the misfortune of possessing a 'bust of Pallas,' never can bear to look at it in the twilight. Our great poet, Mr. Browning, author of 'Paracelsus,' &c., is enthusiastic in his admiration of the rhythm."

Poe himself, although extremely proud of the profound impression " The Raven " had made on the public,
had no particular fondness for it, and preferred, far
more, many of his juvenile pieces ; they, he could not
but feel, were the offspring of inspiration, whilst this
was but the product of art—of art, of course, control-
ling and controlled by genius.   Writing to a favourite
correspondent upon this subject, he remarks :—

" What you say about the blundering criticism of ' the
*Hartford Review* man ' is just.   For the purposes of poetry it
is quite sufficient that a thing is possible, or at least that
the improbability be not offensively glaring.   It is true that
in several ways, as you say, the lamp might have thrown the
bird's shadow on the floor.   *My* conception was that of the
bracket candelabrum affixed against the wall, high up above
the door and bust, as is often seen in the English palaces,
and even in some of the better houses of New York.

" Your objection to the *tinkling* of the footfalls is far more
pointed, and in the course of composition occurred so forcibly
to myself that I hesitated to use the term.   I finally used it,
because I saw that it had, in its first conception, been suggested to my mind by the sense of the *supernatural* with
which it was, at the moment, filled.   No human or physical
foot could tinkle on a soft carpet, therefore, the tinkling of
feet would vividly convey the supernatural impression.   This
was the idea, and it is good within itself ; but if it fails, (as
I fear it does,) to make itself immediately and generally *felt*,
according to my intention, then in so much is it badly con-
veyed, or expressed.

" Your appreciation of ' The Sleeper ' delights me.   In the

higher qualities of poetry it is better than ' The Raven ; ' but
there is not one man in a million who could be brought to
agree with me in this opinion.  ' The Raven,' of course, is
far the better as a work of art ; but in the true basis of all
art, ' The Sleeper ' is the superior.  I wrote the latter when
quite a boy.

" You quote, I think, the two *best* lines in ' The Valley of
Unrest '—those about the palpitating trees."

Whence Poe drew the first idea of " The Raven "
is a much mooted point.  The late Buchanan Read
informed Robert Browning that Poe described to him,
(*i.e.*, Read,) the whole process of the construction of his
poem, and declared that the suggestion of it lay wholly
in a line from " Lady Geraldine's Courtship : "—

" With a murmurous stir uncertain, in the air the purple
curtain," &c.

This account necessarily involves some misunderstanding : that Poe did derive certain hints, unconsciously
or otherwise, from Mrs. Browning's poem cannot be
doubted, as, for instance, in his parallel line to the
above :—

" And the silken, sad, uncertain rustling of each purple
curtain ; "

but the germ of " The Raven " is most assuredly discoverable elsewhere.  Does not the following explanation offer more tangible evidence as to its origin than

anything yet published ? Does it not, indeed, tear the veil from the mystery, and prove that the first suggestion was derived from an American theme ?

It has been seen that in 1843 Poe was writing for the *New Mirror*. The number for October 14th contained some verses entitled " Isadore," by Mr. Albert Pike, a well-known American *littérateur*. Amongst some introductory remarks by the irrepressible editor, N. P. Willis, these words occur : " We do not understand why we should not tell what we chance to know —that these lines were written after sitting up late at study—the thought of losing her who slept near him at his toil having suddenly crossed his mind in the stillness of midnight." This statement really establishes a first coincidence between the poems of Poe and Pike ; both write a poem lamenting a lost love, when, in point of fact, neither one nor the other had lost either his " Isadore," or his " Lenore," save in imagination ; and in his half-hoaxing, half-serious, " Philosophy of Composition " Poe states that the theme adopted for the projected poem was "a lover lamenting his deceased mistress." Far more important, however, than the subject of his verse, so he suggests, was the effect to be obtained from the refrain, and in Mr. Pike's composition the most distinctive—the only salient—feature is the refrain of " forever, Isadore," with which each stanza concludes. A still more remarkable coincidence follows : in his search for a suitable refrain Poe would have his to-be-mystified readers believe that he was irresistibly impelled to select the word " Nevermore." Evidently there are plenty of equally eligible words in the English language—words embodying the long sonorous $\bar{o}$ in connection with $r$ as the most producible consonant; but a perusal of Mr. Pike's poem rendered research needless, for not only does the refrain contain the antithetic word to *never*, and end with the *-ōre* syllable, but in *one* line are found the words " never," and " more," and in others the words " no more," " evermore," and " forever more "—quite sufficient, all must admit, for the analytic mind of Poe.

Thus far the subject, the refrain, and the word selected for the refrain, have been easily paralleled, and over the transmutation of the heroine's name from Isadore into Lenore no words need be wasted. In concluding this section of our argument, it is but just that some specimen of Mr. Pike's work should be shown ; two stanzas, therefore, of his poem—which contains six stanzas fewer than Poe's — shall be cited :—

" Thou art lost to me forever—I have lost thee, Isadore,—
Thy head will never rest upon my loyal bosom more.
Thy tender eyes will never more gaze fondly into mine,
Nor thine arms around me lovingly, and trustingly entwine.
Thou art lost to me forever, Isadore.

"My footsteps through the rooms resound all sadly and
  forlore;
The garish sun shines flauntingly upon the unswept floor;
The mocking-bird still sits and sings a melancholy strain,
For my heart is like a heavy cloud that overflows with rain.
  Thou art lost to me forever, Isadore."

Mr. Pike's metre and rhythm are, as might be
expected, very much less dexterously managed than
Poe's, although the *intention* was evidently to produce
an effect similar to that afterwards carried out in
" The Raven ; " but the irregularities are so eccentric
that one sees that the prototype poem was that of a
writer unable to get beyond the intention—one unacquainted with metrical laws. " Of course, I pretend to
no originality in either the rhythm, or the metre of
' The Raven,' " said Poe, adding, " what originality ' The
Raven,' has, is in their " (the forms of verse employed)
" *combination into stanza,* nothing even remotely approaching this combination has ever been attempted."

But " Isadore " contains no allusion to the " ghastly
grim and ancient Raven," unless its " melancholy
burden " be shadowed forth by the " melancholy
strain " of " the *mocking*-bird." Whence, then, did
Poe import his sable auxiliary, the pretext, as he tells
us, for the natural repetition of the refrain ? " Naturally, a parrot, in the first instance, suggested itself,"
he remarks, and as a favourite work with him was
Gresset's *chef d'œuvre,* it is not improbable that a remi-

niscence of "Ver-Vert"—not "Vert-Vert," as many
persist in miscalling that immortal bird—*may* have
given him the first hint, but that it was in " Barnaby
Rudge " he finally found the needed fowl seems clear
to us.   Upon the conclusion of that story Poe, referring to a prospective review he had formerly published
of it, * called attention to certain points he deemed
Dickens had failed to make : the raven therein, for
instance, he considered, " might have been made more
than we now see it, a portion of the conception of the
fantastic Barnaby.   Its croakings might have been
prophetically heard in the course of the drama.   Its
character might have performed, in regard to that of
the idiot, much the same part as does, in music, the
accompaniment in respect to the air."   Here, indeed,
beyond question, is seen shadowed forth the poet's
own raven and its duty.

A few additional links in the chain may be added.
The story following Mr. Pike's verses in the *New
Mirror* contains, many times repeated, the unusual
name of " Eulalie."   Till the appearance of " The
Raven," for several years Poe had published but one
new poem, " Dreamland," yet in the following July
appeared—in *The American Review*—his " Eulalie," a
poem which, in many passages, closely resembles
" Isadore."   Thus, Mr. Pike speaks of " thy sweet eyes

* *Vide* p. 189.

radiant," and Poe, in "Eulalie," of "the eyes of the radiant girl." Mr. Pike says

> ——" thy face,
> Which thou didst lovingly upturn with pure and trustful gaze,"

and Poe, " dear Eulalie upturns her matron eye ; " and, be it noted, the gaze of both is *upturned* to the moon. There are other points of resemblance between the poems, needless to advert to here, as the genesis of "The Raven" is now, it is presumed, satisfactorily and unanswerably expounded.

This wonderful piece of poetic mechanism underwent, as did, indeed, nearly all of Poe's work, several alterations and revisions after its first publication. The very many more minute of these variations do not call for notice here, but the change made in the latter half of the eleventh stanza, from the original reading of—

> ' So, when Hope he would adjure,
> Stern Despair returned, instead of the sweet Hope he dared adjure,
> That sad answer, " Nevermore " '—

to its present masterly roll of melancholy music, is too radical to be passed by unnoted.

Poe's reputation now rested upon a firm basis. His society was sought for by the *élite* of American society, and the best houses of New York were ready

to proffer a hearty welcome to him who stood even yet on
the brink of poverty, dogged by all its attendant demons.
"Although he had been connected with some of the
leading magazines of the day," remarks Mrs. Whitman, "and had edited for a time with great ability
several successful periodicals, his literary reputation at
the North had been comparatively limited until his
removal to New York, when he became personally
known to a large circle of authors and literary people,
whose interest in his writings was manifestly enhanced
by the perplexing anomalies of his character and by
the singular magnetism of his presence." But it was not
until the publication of his poetic *chef d'œuvre* that he
became a society lion. When "The Raven" appeared,
as this same lady records, Poe one evening electrified
the company assembled at the house of an accomplished poetess in Waverley Place—where a weekly
*réunion* of artists and men of letters was held—by the
recitation, at the request of his hostess, of the wonderful poem.

No longer merely a somewhat-to-be-dreaded reviewer
but now a famous man, it became necessary to include
the poet in the biographical critical laudations of " Our
Contributors," published from time to time in *Graham's
Magazine.* "Edgar Allan Poe" formed the seventeenth
article in the series of American *literati,* so lowly had
his merits been gauged, and to James Russell Lowell

was intrusted the task of adjudicating upon his claims
to a niche in the Pantheon. In many respects
Lowell's critique, published in February 1845, is the
best yet given upon certain characteristics of Poe's
genius, and although the estimate formed of his
poetic precocity is overdrawn, being founded upon
incorrect *data,*—and although the reviewer evidently
lacks sympathy with the reviewed—with the admirable
analysis of our poet's tales, it would be difficult to find
fault. In this article, as originally published—and it
may be remarked that it has since been greatly revised—
Professor Lowell, after styling Poe " the most discrimi-
nating, philosophical, and fearless critic upon imaginative works who has written in America," proceeds to
qualify his remarks by adding :—

He *might be,* rather than he always *is,* for he seems sometimes to mistake his phial of prussic-acid for his inkstand. If
we do not always agree with him in his premises, we are, at
least, satisfied that his deductions are logical, and that we are
reading the thoughts of a man who thinks for himself, and
says what he thinks, and knows well what he is talking
about. . . . We do not know him personally, but we suspect
him for a man who has one or two pet prejudices on which
he prides himself. These sometimes allure him out of the
strict path of criticism, but, where they do not interfere, we
would put almost entire confidence in his judgments. Had
Mr. Poe the control of a magazine of his own, in which
to display his critical abilities, he would have been as auto-
cratic, ere this, in America, as Professor Wilson has been in

England; and his criticisms, we are sure, would have been far more profound and philosophical than those of the Scotchman."

With reference to the poet's career apart from literature, Professor Lowell observes that " Remarkable experiences are usually confined to the inner life of imaginative men, but Mr. Poe's biography displays a vicissitude and peculiarity of interest such as is rarely met with," and he thereupon furnishes a short *résumé* of his hero's adventures. Of Poe's powers as a writer of fiction he remarks :—

" In his tales, he has chosen to exhibit his powers chiefly in that dim region which stretches from the very utmost limits of the probable into the weird confines of superstition and unreality. He combines in a very remarkable manner two faculties which are seldom found united; a power of influencing the mind of the reader by the impalpable shadows of mystery, and a minuteness of detail which does not leave a pin, or a button unnoticed. . . . Even his mystery is mathematical to his own mind. To him $x$ is a known quality. . . . However vague some of his figures may seem, however formless the shadows, to him the outline is as clear and distinct as that of a geometrical diagram. For this reason Mr. Poe has no sympathy with *mysticism.* The mystic dwells *in* the mystery, is enveloped with it; it colours all his thoughts. . . . Mr. Poe, on the other hand, is a spectator *ab extrá.* He analyses, he dissects, he watches

——' with an eye serene
The very pulse of the machine,'

for such it practically is to him, with wheels and cogs and piston-rods all working to produce a certain end. It is this that makes him so good a critic. Nothing baulks him, or throws him off the scent, *except now and then a prejudice.*

"A monomania he paints with great power. He loves to dissect these cancers of the mind, and to trace all the subtle ramifications of its roots. In raising images of horror, also, he has a strange success; conveying to us sometimes by a dusty hint some terrible *doubt* which is the secret of all horror. He leaves to imagination the task of finishing the picture, a task to which only she is competent :—

> "' For much imaginary work was there;
> Conceit deceitful, so compact, so kind,
> That for Achilles' image stood his spear,
> Gripp'd in an armed hand ; himself, behind,
> Was left unseen, save to the eye of mind.' "

Professor Lowell, alluding to the highly finished and classical *form* of Poe's writings, refers, as an example of his style, to "The Fall of the House of Usher," remarking, "It has a singular charm for us, and we think that no one could read it without being strongly moved by its serene and sombre beauty. Had its author written nothing else, it would alone have been enough to stamp him as a man of genius, and the master of a classic style. In this tale occurs one of the most beautiful of his poems " . . . (*i.e.,* " The Haunted Palace ")—" we know no modern poet who might not have been justly proud of it."

The publication of " The Raven " gave an immediate

impetus to Poe's activity, and aided him to dispose of
the result of his labours ; the press teemed with his
work.  The February number of Godey's magazine
contained his " Thousand and Second Tale of Scheheraz-
zade," a satiric story made up chiefly of odds and ends
of scientific wonders, and supposed to relate the ultimate fate of the vizier's daughter, to whom all the
tales in " The Arabian Nights " are ascribed.   The
poet's love of hidden hoaxing is well exemplified by
the names of the personages in this little romance ; for
instance, the heroine is " Scheherazade," (She her has
said,) and the incidents are assumedly derived from the
Oriental work, " Tellmenow Isitsoörnot," (Tell me now
is it so or not,) which is compared, for its rarity, with
the " Zohar," (So ah,) of " Jochaides," (Joke aides.)
These trifles, and similar ones, occurring frequently
in the poet's prose works, are emanations of the spirit
which excelled in, and even delighted at, " The Balloon
Hoax," the " Von Kempelen Discovery," and, in a
higher degree, the analyses of " Marie Roget," the
" Case of M. Valdemar," and others of that genus.

For the *Evening Mirror* of February 3d Poe wrote
an article on " Didacticism," in which he inveighed
strongly against those who deemed poetry a fit medium
for the dissemination of " morals ; " all the more salient
portions of the essay were embodied in subsequent
critiques.  On the 8th of the month he reviewed, in

the *Broadway Journal*, an American selection from the poems of Bulwer, and rated the editor of the book for giving a *selection* only ; he should, he considers, "in common justice, have either given us *all* the poems of the author, or something that should have worn at least the semblance of an argument in objection to the poems omitted," and concludes with the request that in any future edition this editor " will cut out his introduction, and give in place of it the poems of Bulwer which, whether rightfully or wrongfully, have been omitted." "Some Secrets of the Magazine Prison-House " appeared in the *Journal* for the 15th of February, and, undoubtedly, throw a lurid light upon the mysteries of the unfortunate poet's impecuniosity ; that the references *are* to himself no one acquainted with his career can doubt. As this short paper is unknown to many of the poet's admirers, and as it is explanatory of some of the miseries of his life, we give it *in extensô* :—

" The want of an International Copyright Law, by rendering it nearly impossible to obtain anything from the booksellers in the way of remuneration for literary labour, has had the effect of forcing many of our very best writers into the service of the Magazines and Reviews, which, with a pertinacity that does them credit, keep up in a certain or uncertain degree the good old saying that even in the thankless field of Letters the labourer is worthy of his hire. How—by dint of what dogged instinct of the honest and proper—these journals have contrived to persist in their paying practices, in the very teeth of the opposition got up by the Fosters and Leonard Scotts, who furnish for eight dollars any four of the British periodicals for a year, is a point we have had much difficulty in settling to our satisfaction, and we have been forced to settle it at last upon no more reasonable ground than that of a still lingering *esprit de patrie.* That Magazines can live, and not only live but thrive, and not only thrive but afford to disburse money for original contributions, are facts which can only be solved, under the circumstances, by the really fanciful, but still agreeable supposition, that there is somewhere still existing an ember not altogether quenched among the fires of good feeling for letters and literary men that once animated the American bosom.

"It would *not do* (perhaps this is the idea) to let our poor devil authors absolutely starve while we grow fat, in a literary sense, on the good things of which we unblushingly pick the pocket of all Europe: it would not be exactly the thing, *comme il faut,* to permit a positive atrocity of this kind ; and hence we have Magazines, and hence we have a portion of the public who subscribe to these Magazines (through sheer pity), and hence we have Magazine publishers (who sometimes take upon themselves the duplicate title of ' editor *and* proprietor '),—publishers, we say, who, under certain conditions of good conduct, occasional puffs, and decent subserviency at all times, make it a point of conscience to encourage the poor-devil author with a dollar or two, more or less as he behaves himself properly, and abstains from the indecent habit of turning up his nose.

"We hope, however, that we are not so prejudiced, or so vindictive, as to insinuate that what certainly does look like illiberality on the part of them, (the Magazine publishers,) is really an illiberality chargeable to *them.* In fact, it will be seen at once that what we have said has a tendency directly the reverse of any such accusation. These publishers pay *something*—other publishers nothing at all. Here certainly is a difference—although a mathematician might contend that the difference might be infinitesimally small. Still, these Magazine editors and proprietors *pay* (that is the word), and with your true poor-devil author the smallest favours are sure to be thankfully received. No : the illiberality lies at the door of the demagogue-ridden public, who suffer their anointed delegates (or perhaps arointed—which is it ?) to insult the common sense of them (the public) by making orations in our national halls on the beauty and conveniency of robbing the Literary Europe on the highway, and on the gross absurdity in especial of admitting so unprincipled a principle that a man has any right and title either to his own brains, or the flimsy material that he chooses to spin out of them, like a confounded caterpillar as he is. If anything of this gossamer character stands in need of protection, why we have our hands full at once with the silkworms and the *morus multicaulis.*

"But if we cannot, under the circumstances, complain of the absolute illiberality of the Magazine publishers (since pay they do), there is at least one particular in which we have against them good grounds of accusation. Why, (since pay they must,) do they not pay with a good grace and *promptly ?* Were we in an ill-humour at this moment we could a tale unfold which would erect the hair on the head of Shylock. A young author, struggling with Despair itself in the shape of a ghastly poverty, which has no alleviation—no sympathy from an everyday world that cannot understand his necessities, and that would pretend not to understand them if it comprehended them ever so well—this young author is politely requested to compose an article, for which he will ' be handsomely paid.' Enraptured, he neglects perhaps for a month the sole employment which affords him the chance of a livelihood, and having starved through the month (he and his family) completes at length the month of starvation and the article, and despatches the latter, (with a broad hint about the former,) to the pursy ' editor' and bottle-nosed ' proprietor' who has condescended to honour him (the poor devil) with his patronage. A month (starving still), and no reply. Another month — still none. Two months more—still none. A second letter, modestly hinting that the article may not have reached its destination — still no reply. At the expiration of six additional months, personal application is made at the ' editor and proprietor's ' office. Call again. The poor devil goes out, and does not fail to call again. Still call again;—and call again is the word for three or four months more. His patience exhausted, the article is demanded. No—he can't have it—(the truth is, it was too good to be given up so easily)—' it is in print,' and ' contributions of this character are never paid for (it is a *rule* we have) under six months after publication. Call in six months after the issue of your affair, and your money is ready for you—for we are business men ourselves—prompt.' With this the poor devil is satisfied, and makes up his mind that the ' editor and proprietor' is a gentleman, and that of course he (the poor devil) will wait as requested. And it is supposable that he would have waited if he could— but Death in the meantime would not. He dies, and by the good luck of his decease, (which came by starvation,) the fat ' editor and proprietor' is fatter henceforward, and for ever, to the amount of five and twenty dollars, very cleverly saved, to be spent generously in canvas-backs and champagne.

"There are two things which we hope the reader will not do as he runs over this article : first, we hope that he will not believe that we write from any personal experience of our own, for we have only the reports of actual sufferers to depend upon ; and second, that he will not make any personal application of our remarks to any Magazine publisher now living, it being well known that they are all as remarkable for their generosity and urbanity, as for their intelligence and appreciation of Genius."

On Friday, February 28th, Poe delivered a lecture in the Library of the New York Historical Society, on the "Poets and Poetry of America." The discourse attracted much attention, not only on account of the lecturer's eloquence, personal beauty, and the magnetic fascination of his presence, but, also, by the originality and courage of his remarks. He daringly attacked the ephemeral favourites of the day, and did not forbear from vigorous onslaughts upon the editors and compilers who had belauded them into temporary notoriety. The result of this lecture was that the attacked poured forth torrents of abuse, none the less annoying because anonymous, none the less effective because false. A few friends defended the poet in such publications as were open to them : the *American Review* referred to "the devoted spirit in which he advocated the claims and urged the responsibilities of literature. The necessity of a just and independent criticism," says this journal, "was his main topic. He made unmitigated war upon the prevalent Puffery, and dragged several popular idols from their pedestals. His closest critical remarks were given to an examination of the poetry of Mrs. Sigourney and the Davidsons. Bryant, Halleck, and Willis were spoken of briefly, but any neglect in this particular was compensated by several choicely delivered recitations from their verses. . . . There has been a great deal said about this lecture which should be either repeated or printed."

This lecture of the now famous Edgar Poe was a nine-days' wonder, and, on the 8th March following its delivery, the poet himself thus wrote about it :—

" In the late lecture on the ' Poets and Poetry of America,' delivered before an audience made up chiefly of editors and their connections, I took occasion to speak what I know to be the truth, and I endeavoured so to speak it that there should be no chance of misunderstanding what it was I intended to say. I told these gentlemen to their teeth, that, with a *very* few noble exceptions, they had been engaged for many years in a system of indiscriminate laudation of American books—a system which, more than any other one thing in the world, had tended to the depression of that ' American Literature' whose elevation it was designed to effect. I said this, and very much more of a similar tendency, with as thorough a distinctness as I could command. Could I, at the moment, have invented any terms *more* explicit, wherewith to express my contempt of our general editorial course of corruption and puffery, I should have employed them beyond the shadow of a doubt;—and should I think of anything more expressive *hereafter*, I will endeavour either to find or to make an opportunity for its introduction to the public.

"And what, for all this, had I to anticipate? In a very few cases the open, and, in several, the silent approval of the more chivalrous portion of the press;—but in a majority of instances, I should have been weak indeed to look for anything but abuse. To the Willises—the O'Sullivans—the Duyckincks—to the choice and magnanimous few who spoke promptly in my praise, and who have since taken my hand with a more cordial and a more impressive grasp than ever—to these, I return, of course, my acknowledgments, for that they have rendered me my due. To my vilifiers I return also such thanks as they deserve, inasmuch as without what they have done me the honour to say there would have been much of point wanting in the compliments of my friends. Had I, indeed, from the former received any less equivocal tokens of disapprobation, I should at this moment have been looking about me to discover what sad blunder I had committed.

"I am most sincere in what I say. I thank these, my opponents, for their goodwill,—manifested, of course, after their own fashion. No doubt they mean me well—if they could only be brought to believe it; and I shall expect more reasonable things from them hereafter. In the meantime, I await patiently the period when they shall have fairly made an end of what they have to say—when they shall have sufficiently exalted themselves in their own opinion—and when, especially, they shall have brought *me* over to that precise view of the question which it is their endeavour to have me adopt.                                        E. A. P."

As a pleasing pendant to the whirlwind which some portions of this lecture aroused may be mentioned the fact that, during his discourse, Poe had recited, with approving comments, " Florence Vane," a beautiful lyric by Philip P. Cooke, a young Virginian, who died a few years later in his youthful and budding promise of fame. Poe's sympathetic delivery, and the warm encomia he awarded the poem and its author, excited considerable interest, and caused " Florence Vane " to take a place in American literary selections which, however deserved, it might not otherwise so readily have succeeded in obtaining.

On the same day that the above letter was written Poe associated himself with two journalists in the editorial management of the *Broadway Journal.* In consequence of this new undertaking, the poet resigned the position he had held on the *Evening Mirror,* but, in bidding farewell to its wretched drudgery, he entered into trials and troubles almost as bad, and commenced a series of episodes not only as romantic, but, also, quite as unfortunate, as the earlier years of his life.

END OF VOL. I.

PRINTED BY BALLANTYNE, HANSON AND CO.
EDINBURGH AND LONDON

CPSIA information can be obtained at www.ICGtesting.com
Printed in the USA
BVOW03s1020301013

335002BV00018B/749/P